CHARLES R. SWINDOLL

SWINDOLL'S
NEW TESTAMENT
INSIGHTS

INSIGHTS ON
ROMANS 6 – 8

ZONDERVAN®

ZONDERVAN.com/
AUTHORTRACKER
follow your favorite authors

ZONDERVAN

Insights on Romans Sampler
Copyright © 2009 by Charles R. Swindoll

Zondervan, *Grand Rapids, Michigan 49530*

ISBN 978-0-310-61444-9

Published in association with Yates & Yates, www.yates2.com.

Cover and interior design by Sherri Hoffman

Printed in the United States of America

CONTENTS

SPECIAL FEATURES

Key Terms (word studies)

Maps

Timelines

Pictures

Charts

Sidebars

From My Journal

Application section

INSIGHT FOR LIVING
SPECIAL EDITION

You probably won't find a more profound and practical section of New Testament Scripture than Romans 6–8. In our world of disappointment, selfishness, and moral compromise, this is the stuff every Christian desperately needs to know . . . by heart. It's the stuff of victory.

These three chapters stand out in the book of Romans like a magnificent peak in an already majestic mountain range of spiritual truth. Is there anything more refreshing than Paul's description in Romans 6 of our freedom from sin's power? Furthermore, we would be hard-pressed to find a clearer discussion of a Christian's ongoing struggle with sin than Romans 7. And Romans 8 comforts us with God's provision of His Spirit and the promises of victory in the inseparable love of Christ. What a powerful section of Scripture!

To express our gratitude for your gift to Insight for Living, we've made this excerpt on Romans 6–8 available to you. We have lifted these pages from my new commentary, *Swindoll's New Testament Insights: Insights on Romans.* The commentary seeks to take the profound content of Paul's letter and present it in a fresh and easy-to-read way, in light of today's needs.

As you work your way up this marvelous mountainside in the midst of Paul's letter to the Romans, keep in mind that your climb to the stunning vista on the peak of Romans 8 may feel daunting. But for those who remain diligent in pursuing truth, God will turn the key to your understanding and open wide the doors of your heart . . . just as He's done in mine.

Chuck Swindoll

Charles R. Swindoll

AUTHOR'S PREFACE

For almost sixty years I have loved the Bible. It was that love for the Scriptures, mixed with a clear call into the gospel ministry during my tour of duty in the Marine Corps, that resulted in my going to Dallas Theological Seminary to prepare for a lifetime of ministry. During those four great years I had the privilege of studying under outstanding men of God, who also loved God's Word. They not only held the inerrant Word of God in high esteem, they taught it carefully, preached it passionately, and modeled it consistently. A week never passes without my giving thanks to God for the grand heritage that has been mine to claim! I am forever indebted to those fine theologians and mentors, who cultivated in me a strong commitment to the understanding, exposition, and application of God's truth.

For more than forty-five years I have been engaged in doing just that—*and how I love it!* I confess without hesitation that I am addicted to the examination and the proclamation of the Scriptures. Because of this, books have played a major role in my life for as long as I have been in ministry—especially those volumes that explain the truths and enhance my understanding of what God has written. Through these many years I have collected a large personal library, which has proven invaluable as I have sought to remain a faithful student of the Bible. To the end of my days, my major goal in life is to communicate the Word with accuracy, insight, clarity, and practicality. Without resourceful and reliable books to turn to, I would have "run dry" decades ago.

Among my favorite and most well-worn volumes are those that have enabled me to get a better grasp of the biblical text. Like most expositors, I am forever searching for literary tools that I can use to hone my gifts and sharpen my skills. For me, that means finding resources that make the complicated simple and easy to understand, that offer insightful comments and word pictures that enable me to see the relevance of sacred truth in light of my twenty-first-century world, and that drive those truths home to my heart in ways I do not easily forget. When I come across such books, they wind up in my hands as I devour them and then place them in my library for further reference ... and, believe me, I often return to them. What a relief it is to have these resourceful works to turn to when I lack fresh insight, or when I need just the right story or illustration, or when I get stuck in the tangled text and cannot find my way out. For the serious expositor, a library is essential. As a mentor of mine once said, *"Where else can you have 10,000 professors at your fingertips?"*

In recent years I have discovered there are not nearly enough resources like those I just described. It was such a discovery that prompted me to consider becoming a part of the answer instead of lamenting the problem. But the solution would result in a huge undertaking. A writing project that covers all of the books and letters of the New Testament seemed overwhelming and intimidating. A rush of relief came when I realized that during the past forty-five-plus years I've taught and preached through most of the New Testament. In my files were folders filled with notes from those messages that were just lying there, waiting to be brought out of hiding, given a fresh and relevant touch in light of today's needs, and applied to fit into the lives of men and women who long for a fresh word from the Lord. *That did it!* I began to pursue the best publisher to turn my dream into reality.

Thanks to the hard work of my literary agents, Sealy and Matt Yates, I located a publisher interested in taking on a project this extensive. I thank the fine people at Zondervan Publishing House for their enthusiastic support of this multivolume venture that will require over ten years to complete. Having met most of them over the years through other written works I've authored, I knew they were qualified to handle such an undertaking and would be good stewards of my material, staying with the task of getting all of it into print. I am grateful for the confidence and encouragement of both Stan Gundry and Paul Engle, who have remained loyal and helpful from the beginning. It is also a pleasure to work alongside Verlyn Verbrugge; I sincerely appreciate his seasoned wisdom and keen-eyed assistance.

It has also been especially delightful to work, again, with my longtime friend and former editor, John Sloan. He has provided invaluable counsel as my general editor. Best of all has been John's enthusiastic support. I must also express my gratitude to both Mark Gaither and Mike Svigel for their tireless and devoted efforts, serving as my hands-on, day-to-day editors. They have done superb work as we have walked our way through the verses and chapters of all twenty-seven New Testament books. It has been a pleasure to see how they have taken my original material and helped me shape it into a style that remains true to the text of the Scriptures, at the same time interestingly and creatively developed, and all the while allowing my voice to come through in a natural and easy-to-read manner.

I need to add sincere words of appreciation to the congregations I have served in various parts of these United States for almost five decades. It has been my good fortune to be the recipient of their love, support, encouragement, patience, and frequent words of affirmation as I have fulfilled my calling to stand and deliver God's message year after year. The sheep from all those flocks have endeared themselves to this shepherd in more ways than I can put into words ... and none more than those I currently serve with delight at Stonebriar Community Church in Frisco, Texas.

Finally, I must thank my wife, Cynthia, for her understanding of my addiction to studying, to preaching, and to writing. Never has she discouraged me from staying at it. Never has she failed to urge me in the pursuit of doing my very best. On the contrary, her affectionate support personally, and her own commitment to excellence in leading *Insight for Living* for more than three decades, have combined to keep me faithful to my calling "in season and out of season." Without her devotion to me and apart from our mutual partnership throughout our lifetime of ministry together, *Swindoll's New Testament Insights* would never have been undertaken.

I am grateful that it has now found its way into your hands and, ultimately, onto the shelves of your library. My continued hope and prayer is that you will find these volumes helpful in your own study and personal application of the Bible. May they help you come to realize, as I have over these many years, that God's Word is as timeless as it is true.

The grass withers, the flower fades,
but the word of our God stands forever. (Isaiah 40:8)

Chuck Swindoll
Frisco, Texas

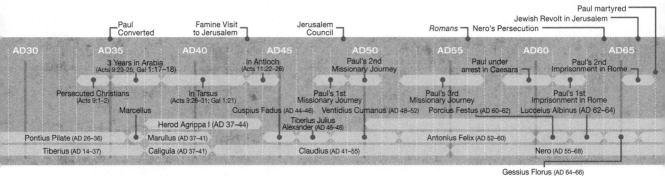

Paul martyred

Jewish Revolt in Jerusalem

Paul Converted   Famine Visit to Jerusalem   Jerusalem Council   *Romans*   Nero's Persecution

AD30   AD35   AD40   AD45   AD50   AD55   AD60   AD65

3 Years in Arabia (Acts 9:23-25; Gal 1:17-18)   In Antioch (Acts 11:22-26)   Paul's 2nd Missionary Journey   Paul under arrest in Caesara   Paul's 2nd Imprisonment in Rome

Persecuted Christians (Acts 9:1-2)   In Tarsus (Acts 9:26-31; Gal 1:21)   Paul's 1st Missionary Journey   Paul's 3rd Missionary Journey   Paul's 1st Imprisonment in Rome

Marcellus   Cuspius Fadus (AD 44-46)   Ventidius Cumanus (AD 48-52)   Porcius Festus (AD 60-62)   Lucceius Albinus (AD 62-64)

Tiberius Julius Alexander (AD 46-48)

Herod Agrippa I (AD 37-44)

Pontius Pilate (AD 26-36)   Marullus (AD 37-41)   Antonius Felix (AD 52-60)

Tiberius (AD 14-37)   Caligula (AD 37-41)   Claudius (AD 41-55)   Nero (AD 55-68)

Gessius Florus (AD 64-66)

3rd miss. journey

Planned visit to Rome

0   50 km.

0   50 miles

After returning to Israel from his third missionary journey, Paul visited the church leaders in Jerusalem to share the results of his ministry. Then, perhaps after a short visit with his friends in Antioch, Paul planned to sail for Rome, where he would launch his mission to the western frontier of Spain. But, as had been foretold, Paul was arrested (Acts 20:22–23). He would eventually journey to Rome ... in chains.

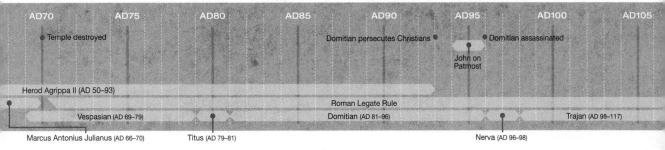

AD70   AD75   AD80   AD85   AD90   AD95   AD100   AD105

Temple destroyed   Domitian persecutes Christians ●   ● Domitian assassinated

John on Patmost

Herod Agrippa II (AD 50–93)

Roman Legate Rule

Vespasian (AD 69–79)   Domitian (AD 81–96)   Trajan (AD 98–117)

Marcus Antonius Julianus (AD 66–70)   Titus (AD 79–81)   Nerva (AD 96–98)

ROMANS

Introduction

Travel back in time with me. Let's go back to the winter of AD 57. We're at a narrow land bridge between mainland Greece and the Peloponnese, where a Roman city rakes in fortunes from heavy-laden ships and cash-heavy tourists. Outside the city, in the home of a wealthy and hospitable Christian named Gaius, two men discuss a scroll. One paces the room, pouring out his thoughts to the other, who sits at a large table, taking copious notes.

The speaker walks with a deliberate strength, although his shoulders are rounded and a noticeable hitch interrupts his gait. His arms and face bear the marks of wind, sun, age, and mistreatment. His fingers are knotted and curled and fused in an unnatural angle, the telltale sign of multiple stonings. You would expect that a body such as this would contain a broken, demoralized spirit, but the eyes reveal something different. They flash with energy and sparkle with the optimism of a teenager about to get his driver's license.

The city is Corinth. The one pacing the floor is Paul; his amanuensis at the table, Tertius. The document they are preparing will eventually become the apostle's letter to the church in Rome, the most significant piece of literature the Lord would ever commission His most prolific evangelist to write. Little does Paul or anyone realize the impact it will have through the centuries to come. From [Origen of Alexandria] in the [third century] to Barnhouse of Philadelphia in the twentieth, countless theologians will pen innumerable pages of exposition and meditation from the apostle's magnum opus. Augustine will find the seed plot of his

Major Themes of Romans

Section	Salutation	The Wrath of God	The Grace of God
Themes	Paul's calling and plans The identity of Christ The gospel Faith "Righteousness of God"	"Righteousness of God" The moral failure of humanity God's judicial abandonment of humanity Humanity's hopelessness and eternal peril	"Righteousness of God" Powerlessness of Works Justification through Faith Grace/Free Gift Reconciliation
Key Terms	Apostle Gospel Faith Salvation Righteousness	Unrighteousness Judge Law Wrath Hand over	Justify Works/Law Circumcision Propitiation Grace
Passage	1:1–17	1:18–3:20	3:21–5:21

The Faithfulness of God	The Majesty of God	The Righteousness of God	Conclusion
Righteousness	Righteousness through faith	Love	Gentiles
The futility of human effort	Israel in the plan of God	Civic responsibility	The gospel
The necessity of the Holy Spirit	The justice of God	Unity	Paul's past
Children/heirs of God	The sovereignty of God	Mutual judgment	Paul's future
Assurance of future "glory"	The plan of God	Mutual acceptance	
		Joy, peace, and hope	
"Flesh"	Mercy	Conform	Obedience
Spirit	Harden	Transform	Commend
Sanctification	Remnant	Prove	Dissention
Predestined	Mystery	Accept	Hindrance
Glorified			
6:1–8:39	9:1–11:36	12:1–15:13	15:14–16:27

faith in this letter. This document will spark a revolution in the heart of Martin Luther, who will reintroduce the truth of justification by grace alone, through faith alone, in Christ alone—a doctrine all but obscured by the dogma of men who stood to profit from a false gospel of works. It will ignite the mind of Jonathan Edwards, strangely warm the heart of John Wesley, and fuel the revival fire of George Whitefield.

"CALLED AS AN APOSTLE, SET APART FOR THE GOSPEL OF GOD" (1:1)

Paul's journey to this place and time has been a winding one. Though born in the cosmopolitan hubbub of Tarsus, Paul matured in the shadow of the great temple in Jerusalem. Within its enormous, gleaming white walls, he learned at the feet of the famous rabbi Gamaliel (Acts 22:3). Though a Roman citizen (22:25–28), he

In three missionary journeys, spanning no less than fifteen years, Paul labored to evangelize the empire east of Rome—an incredibly dangerous and arduous ministry. Nevertheless, when most would retire, Paul set his sights on the untamed frontier west of Rome: northern Italy, southern France, Spain, and Portugal.

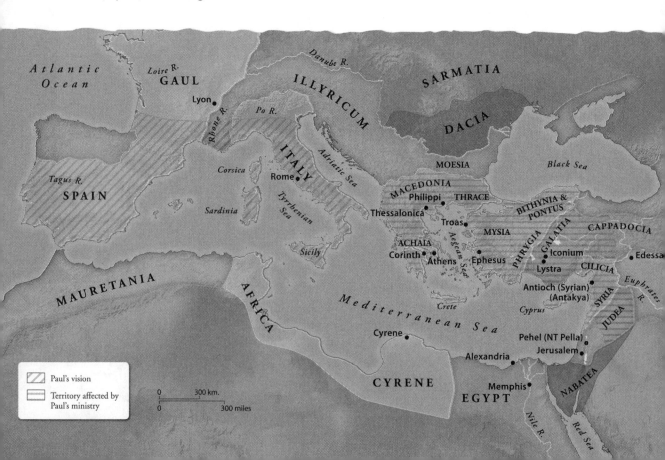

was first and foremost "a son of the covenant." He heard of the great privileges and responsibilities God had given his kindred people. He studied the law of Moses and devoted himself to fulfilling every letter of tradition. And he immersed himself in the inveterate rituals of the Pharisees with a singular goal in mind. He wanted to become like the temple itself: sacred, strong, undefiled, a worthy vessel for the righteousness of God.

But, as often happens in the lives of great men, Paul's zealous pursuit of righteousness took an unexpected turn. While on the road to Damascus in order to silence and persecute Christians, Jesus Christ confronted him, rebuked him, changed him, and then set him on a whole new course (Acts 9:3–22). The righteousness he coveted could not be found in the traditions of the Pharisees, but in the faith of the very people he sought to kill. They would show their former persecutor supernatural grace, first by embracing him, the man who had supervised the stoning of their beloved Stephen (7:58–8:1), and then by showing him the source of their goodness. They were merely passing on the righteousness they had received by grace through faith in Jesus Christ (9:13–19).

Paul's encounter with the risen Christ transformed him. His future lay not in Jerusalem and works of the law, but out among the Gentiles, preaching grace and living by faith. Instead of stamping out Christianity, he would become a tireless apostle, traveling more than twenty thousand miles between Jerusalem and Rome and proclaiming the gospel wherever ears had never heard it. Then, near the end of his third missionary journey, after what many would consider a full life in ministry, the apostle looked westward to the frontier beyond Rome (Rom. 15:24).

"FULL OF GOODNESS, FILLED WITH ALL KNOWLEDGE AND ABLE ALSO TO ADMONISH" (15:14)

Paul had long admired the congregation in the capital city of the empire. Although he had neither founded the church in Rome nor even visited it, he shared close connections with several leading members (Rom. 16:1–15). Many had been his partners in ministry, some were cell mates in the early days of evangelism, several were the fruit of his labors in other regions. Their obedience to the Word and faithfulness to one another had become legendary among the other churches (16:19). This could not have been easy, given their unique pressures in Rome.

During the reign of Emperor Claudius (AD 41–54), the Roman government—normally tolerant of other religions—began to prohibit proselytizing. Claudius likely expelled the Jews from Rome (Acts 18:2) because Jewish Christians had been evangelizing their neighbors. But within a few years, Claudius was poisoned and his adopted heir, Nero, took his place on the throne, and he allowed Jews and Christians to return. After reclaiming their homes and reestablishing their district, the Jewish community undoubtedly pressured Christians to keep a low profile to avoid more trouble. For the first three years of Nero's reign, all was quiet. The teenaged emperor was too occupied with threats within the palace to notice much going on outside. It was during this time that Paul wrote his brothers and sisters in the capital city. Within a few months, however, Nero eliminated the source of internal danger by poisoning his mother. Then he turned his attention to winning the hearts of Roman citizens with grand festivals and massive gladiatorial spectacles.

At the time of Paul's writing, the population of Rome exceeded one million inhabitants, nearly half of whom were bond-servants and recently freed slaves. And, like modern metropolitan centers, Rome was a wonderful place to live for the elite, but challenging for everyone else. The divide between the rich and poor constantly kept city officials on edge as the lower classes were never far from rioting. Most of them lived amid rampant street crime in squalid, high-rise apartment buildings, as tall as five or six stories, with no sanitation or water available above the first floor.

The great divide between the picturesque villas of the privileged and the crime-ridden slums that comprised most of the city left the residents to fend for themselves, which they did by congregating according to race. In other words, first-century Rome was not unlike New York City during the nineteenth and twentieth centuries. Ethnic neighborhoods became governments unto themselves, vying for dominance while maintaining an uneasy peace with one another to avoid persecution by the government (Acts 18:2).

Life was hard for everyone, but being a Christian in that environment made it even worse. For both Jewish and Gentile Christians, the price of discipleship often meant the loss of family and clan, including the safety they provided. They must have felt like squirrels living among angry giants, any one of whom might decide to crush them on a whim. By AD 64, their feelings proved to be justified. Nero went mad. His persecution of the Christians became so shockingly brutal that citizens actually began to pity them. Some say the crime of the Christians that sent them to their deaths was the burning of Rome, but according to the Roman historian, Tacitus, Christians were punished "not so much for the imputed crime of burning Rome, as for their hate and enmity to human kind."[1]

This general impression of Christians—regardless of how unfair or slanderous it was—would factor heavily into the apostle's practical advice near the end of his letter.

"MAY THE GOD OF HOPE FILL YOU WITH ALL JOY AND PEACE IN BELIEVING" (15:13)

The believers in Rome desperately needed encouragement, which this divinely inspired letter provided in three ways.

First, *the letter confirmed their understanding of the gospel and clarified what might have been confusing.* Persecution combined with isolation can cause even the most resilient mind to lose its grip on the truth. In fact, pain and seclusion are the principle tools used in the cruel art of mind control. Prisoners of war report that after several hours of torture, the human mind will accept any absurdity as absolute truth in order to end suffering.

In careful detail and with compelling clarity, Paul explained the truth of the gospel. He drew upon his formal training and the best rhetorical style of the day to present the truth of God in logical sequence. He recalled his years of preaching in synagogues and debating in markets to answer every relevant objection. And, of course, the Holy Spirit inspired the content, superintended the process of writing, and safeguarded the document from error. The believers in Rome received a complete, comprehensive, and concise proclamation of Christian truth. And the effect must have been incredibly calming.

Second, *the letter affirmed the authenticity of their faith and commended them for their obedience.* People on a long and arduous journey frequently need confirmation they are on the right course and should continue as they have been; otherwise they will grow discouraged and reduce their efforts or wander off-course. The church in Rome had long been an exemplary model of steadfast faith and authentic community. Paul encouraged them, in effect, "Keep doing what you have been doing. You're right on target!" Furthermore, the congregation in Rome, like every other church in the first century, was susceptible to the influence of false teachers. This letter equipped them to recognize the truth and to leave no room for heresy.

Third, *the letter cast a vision for the future and urged them to become Paul's partners in accomplishing it.* When churches take their eyes off the horizon, the inevitable result is what can be called a "survival mentality." Rather than accomplishing the plans of God to redeem and transform His creation, they forget their reason for being, which begins a long, agonizing slide into irrelevance. Irrelevant churches fret over inconsequential matters, nitpick their leadership, criticize one another, experiment with worldly strategies for growth, and chase vain philosophies. Meanwhile their surrounding communities hear little of Christ, and what they do hear is unattractive. Paul challenged the believers in Rome with an enormous undertaking: evangelization of the newly expanded empire to the west. It was a landmass greater than what the apostle had covered in three missionary journeys, although not nearly as tame.

THE GOSPEL OF CHRIST AND THE *PAX ROMANA*

Historians call the first two centuries of Roman rule after the birth of Christ, the *Pax Romana* — that is, the "Roman Peace." It was peaceful in that Rome focused less on foreign conquest and more on stabilizing the lands they already ruled, but it was nevertheless a brutal peace. The Empire could quickly mobilize large armies anywhere between Rome and Persia and typi- cally responded to insurrection with shocking cruelty. Once a revolt had been quelled, it was not uncommon for the survivors to be crucified along the roads leading into the region as a warning to new colonists.

While this "peace" was not without bloodshed, it nevertheless paved the way for Paul's evangelistic ministry ... literally. To quickly move troops and commerce around the realm, the Roman government constructed an elaborate highway system, paved with stone and concrete, and regularly patrolled these roads to prevent robbery. This gave the apostle and his entourage unprecedented access to the world as they knew it. And he made the most of his opportunity, circling the Eastern Empire three times in fifteen years and logging more than twenty thousand miles, mostly on government paving and government-con- trolled shipping lanes.

In the end, the merciless "peace" of Rome became the means of a merciful "peace with God" (5:1) for innumerable Gen- tiles during Paul's lifetime, and for countless generations thereafter.

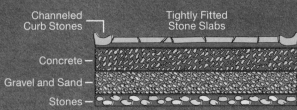

Channeled Curb Stones — Tightly Fitted Stone Slabs

Concrete —
Gravel and Sand —
Stones —

"FOR IN IT THE RIGHTEOUSNESS OF GOD IS REVEALED FROM FAITH TO FAITH" (1:17)

Paul's letter to the believers in Rome can be called many things. Clearly, this became his magnum opus. It is the first systematic theology of the Christian faith. This letter may be considered the believer's constitution—the Christian Magna Carta. We might even call it a manifesto of the new kingdom, for it not only declares our essential beliefs, it establishes our agenda as Christ's disciples. But more than anything, the words Paul and his amanuensis, Tertius, penned twenty centuries ago are no less than the revealed Word of God. Through human agency, the Almighty Creator has breathed out, revealing a grand plan.

"The plan of salvation" outlined in this letter to Christians living in first-century Rome has more than the rescue of individuals in view. The plan of God is more than a mere fire escape through which a few find safety from the flames of eternal punishment. This grand plan—of which all are invited to become a part—is nothing less than the Creator's intention to bring His creation back under divine dominion, to cleanse it of evil, to redeem, reclaim, and renovate the universe so that it, again, reflects His glory. The plan of salvation is good news to each individual, but the greater news is the return of God's righteousness to its rightful place in the world. Some day in the future, Christ will tear the veil between heaven and earth, and the righteousness of God will sweep the "prince of the power of the air" (Eph. 2:2) from his stolen throne, and will again rule over creation. This future is inevitable because God's plan is unstoppable.

In the meantime, the righteousness of God lives in the hearts of those who have received His grace through faith in His Son, Jesus Christ. Therefore, each individual reading Paul's letter to the Romans must answer two questions. First, will you allow God's transformation of the world to begin with you? As Paul will explain, this is not an invitation to try harder, but a plea to submit to His grace before it's too late. Second, if the righteousness of God lives within you now, will you keep it hidden? If you lack knowledge, read on. The book of Romans will explain all you need to know. If you lack courage, this exhortation from an intrepid apostle to a beleaguered church in first-century Rome will revive and reinvigorate your confidence.

Whatever your situation, wherever you happen to be in your spiritual journey, I am convinced that the time you invest in a careful study of this letter will change you forever. This has been true of generations past, and the power of God's Word has not diminished over time. As you read, the Holy Spirit has pledged to provide whatever you lack. You need only believe His promise. If you submit to these truths, then you too will discover, as did Paul, that "the righteous [one] shall live by faith" (1:17).

NOTES: Romans Introduction

1. Tacitus, *The Works of Tacitus*, 2nd ed. (London: Woodward and Peele, 1737), 2:698.

THE FAITHFULNESS OF GOD (ROMANS 6:1 – 8:39)

On September 22, 1862, President Abraham Lincoln issued a proclamation, which began:

> On the first day of January, in the year of our Lord one thousand eight hundred and sixty-three, all persons held as slaves within any State or designated part of a State, the people whereof shall then be in rebellion against the United States, shall be then, thenceforward, and forever free.

The Union would have to fight for many months before slaves in the South could claim their precious freedom. Booker T. Washington was nine when emancipation reached his plantation in southwest Virginia, a day he recalled in his autobiography, *Up from Slavery*:

> The most distinct thing that I now recall in connection with the scene was that some man who seemed to be a stranger (a United States officer, I presume) made a little speech and then read a rather long paper — the Emancipation Proclamation, I think. After the reading we were told that we were all free, and could go when and where we pleased. My mother, who was standing by my side, leaned over and kissed her children, while tears of joy ran down her cheeks. She explained to us what it all meant, that this was the day for which she had been so long praying, but fearing that she would never live to see.[1]

In time, after the final surrender of the Confederacy, the assassination of a president, and a difficult political fight, the States ratified the Thirteenth Amendment, which officially abolished slavery in America. On December 18, 1865, the news swept across Capitol Hill, and down the Shenandoah, over the Appalachians, along the back roads of the Carolinas, deep into the plantations of Georgia, Alabama, Mississippi, and Louisiana, and into the cotton fields of Texas and Arkansas. The word was out: Slaves are free ... at least officially. The practicality of freedom was another matter.

> The wild rejoicing on the part of the emancipated coloured people lasted but for a brief period, for I noticed that by the time they returned to their cabins there was a change in their feelings. The great responsibility of being free, of having charge of themselves, of having to think and plan for themselves and their children, seemed to take possession of them. It was very much like suddenly turning a youth of ten or twelve years out into the world to provide for himself. In a few hours the

great questions with which the Anglo-Saxon race had been grappling for centuries had been thrown upon these people to be solved. These were the questions of a home, a living, the rearing of children, education, citizenship, and the establishment and support of churches. Was it any wonder that within a few hours the wild rejoicing ceased and a feeling of deep gloom seemed to pervade the slave quarters? To some it seemed that, now that they were in actual possession of it, freedom was a more serious thing than they had expected to find it. Some of the slaves were seventy or eighty years old; their best days were gone. They had no strength with which to earn a living in a strange place and among strange people, even if they had been sure where to find a new place of abode. To this class the problem seemed especially hard. Besides, deep down in their hearts there was a strange and peculiar attachment to "old Marster" and "old Missus," and to their children, which they found it hard to think of breaking off. With these they had spent in some cases nearly a half-century, and it was no light thing to think of parting. Gradually, one by one, stealthily at first, the older slaves began to wander from the slave quarters back to the "big house" to have a whispered conversation with their former owners as to the future.[2]

After a brief celebration, many former slaves returned to the fields to continue their servitude as "sharecroppers." Though officially free to go anywhere, little changed for them in a practical sense. Legal emancipation merely presented slaves with the opportunity to live as free men and women. Turning their legal status into actual experience would require an internal transformation. Those who found this challenge too daunting chose the uncomfortable familiarity of slavery instead.

How foolish this appears from the perspective of people who have never known slavery. Yet, Christians—I would say the majority of them—choose slavery over freedom every day. Having been set free, for them to live as free men and women comes neither easily nor naturally. It's a process and, like salvation, it must be accomplished supernaturally. Theologians have given a name to the gradual, internal transformation of a newly freed slave of sin into a fully mature and completely free individual. That term is "sanctification." That is the subject of this section of Paul's letter to the Romans.

Dying to Live (Romans 6:1–14)

[1]What shall we say then? Are we to continue in sin so that grace may increase? [2]May it never be! How shall we who died to sin still live in it? [3]Or do you not know that all of us who have been baptized into Christ Jesus have been baptized into His death? [4]Therefore we have been buried with

KEY TERMS

ἁγιασμός [*hagiasmos*] (*38*) "sanctification, consecration, holiness"

This was a common word in pagan worship, describing anything that was cleansed, set aside for specific use in the worship of a particular god, and therefore ceremonially pure. The Jews used the term in reference to anything reserved for God's use, including the Hebrew race. Paul gave the term an even greater personal application. Because the Holy Spirit dwells within the believer, the believer is a temple and, therefore, no less consecrated than "the Most Holy Place" (Ex. 26:33–34; Lev. 16:2).

σάρξ [*sarx*] (*4561*) "flesh, the physical aspect of humanity"

It was not uncommon for Paul to adopt a secular Greek term and add to its usual meaning to describe a complex spiritual truth. For the apostle, *sarx* was not merely the material aspect of humanity; it stood for our sinful, rebellious manner of thought and deed that permeates the perverted world system after the Fall (Gen. 3:14–19). *Sarx* is that part of our preconversion nature that opposes God's new kingdom manner of thought and deed.

πνεῦμα [*pneuma*] (*4151*) "spirit, the immaterial aspect of humanity, Holy Spirit"

Pneuma literally means "wind" or "breath," but was more commonly used in secular Greek literature to speak of a person's immaterial aspect — that which ceased to exist after death, or continued to live apart from the body. Paul used *pneuma* similarly, but also used the term in reference to God's Holy Spirit. Furthermore, the "Spirit" was not only the third person of the Trinity; the term also represented the mindset of God as opposed to the fallen manner of life in the world. "Spirit" is the opposite of *sarx*.

προορίζω [*proorizō*] (4309) "to determine beforehand, to decide in advance, preordain"

While Paul was not opposed to giving common Greek words a specialized or technical meaning, he more often used their normal, lexical definition. This word simply means "to determine beforehand." While the verb assumes foreknowledge, it does not suggest how knowledge of the future impacts decision-making, if it does at all.

δοξάζω [*doxazō*] (*1392*) "to glorify, to make glorious, to render excellent, to reveal the worth of something"

In the Greek translation of the Old Testament, God's *doxa* is usually a physical manifestation of His holy, righteous nature, which humanity may observe at great risk of death (Ex. 33:18–23). In the New Testament, "the emphasis shifts to participation"[3] whereby the believer shares the glory of Christ (Rom. 8:17; Col. 1:27; 3:4) and eventually receives a resurrected body like His (Phil. 3:21). In the vocabulary of heaven, *doxa* is righteousness made visible.

Him through baptism into death, so that as Christ was raised from the dead through the glory of the Father, so we too might walk in newness of life. [5]For if we have become united with *Him* in the likeness of His death, certainly we shall also be *in the likeness* of His resurrection, [6]knowing this, that our old self was crucified with *Him*, in order that our body of sin might be done away with, so that we would no longer be slaves to sin; [7]for he who has died is freed from sin.

[8]Now if we have died with Christ, we believe that we shall also live with Him, [9]knowing that Christ, having been raised from the dead, is never to die again; death no longer is master over Him. [10]For the death that He died, He died to sin once for all; but the life that He lives, He lives to God. [11]Even so consider yourselves to be dead to sin, but alive to God in Christ Jesus. [12]Therefore do not let sin reign in your mortal body so that you obey its lusts, [13]and do not go on presenting the members of your body to sin *as* instruments of unrighteousness; but present yourselves to God as those alive from the dead, and your members *as* instruments of righteousness to God. [14]For sin shall not be master over you, for you are not under law but under grace.

DO YOU REALLY EXPECT AN ANSWER?

A rhetorical question is really a statement in the form of a query, so it doesn't expect an actual response. That makes it a particularly effective tool in the art of debate. In addition to making a strong point, the rhetorical question appears to put the opponent in the position of having no answer and therefore no response. For example, someone might seal an argument by asking, "You don't expect me to betray my principles, do you?"

Paul undoubtedly faced a number of such situations in his travels across the Roman Empire, and he includes some of them in his letter to the Romans as if to anticipate common objections. These questions do not reflect his teaching on the matter; they merely give him an opportunity to respond. He frequently introduces a rhetorical question with the phrase, "What then?" before responding with an explanation of sound doctrine.

Here are several examples (emphasis added):

Then what advantage has the Jew? Or what is the benefit of circumcision? (3:1)

What then? If some did not believe, their unbelief will not nullify the faithfulness of God, will it? (3:3)

What then? Are we better than they? (3:9)

Where then is boasting? It is excluded. By what kind of law? Of works? (3:27)

What then shall we say that Abraham, our forefather according to the flesh, has found? (4:1)

What shall we say **then**? Are we to continue in sin so that grace may increase? (6:1)

What then? Shall we sin because we are not under law but under grace? May it never be! (6:15)

What shall we say **then**? Is the Law sin? (7:7)

What shall we say **then**? There is no injustice with God, is there? (9:14)

"There ain't no such thing as a free lunch."
"Eat, drink, and be merry, for tomorrow we die."
"Keep your friends close and your enemies closer."
"Let the buyer beware."
"You get what you pay for."
"God helps those who help themselves."

What passes for worldly wisdom is usually bad theology. That's because the world stopped working the way God intended soon after Adam's disobedience dragged the rest of creation into rebellion with him. Consequently, the order and beauty that once graced God's creation, while not completely obliterated, has become twisted and grotesque. Now, the world operates according to a different system, one that leaves little or no room for such heavenly qualities as humility, selflessness, faith, or, the most alien of all, grace.

As Paul concluded the last section, he boldly declared that whereas sin reigned over the earth and death through sin, Jesus Christ had initiated a takeover. To use his words: "Grace multiplied … so that just as sin reigned in death, so also grace will reign through righteousness to eternal life through Jesus Christ our Lord" (5:20–21 NET). This summarizes what he will explain in chapters 6–8.

To begin his explanation, the apostle asks two questions that illustrate how alien grace is to a world dominated by death and to minds given over to depravity. These are two questions for which he already has answers:

"Are we to continue in sin so that grace may increase?" (6:1)
"Shall we sin because we are not under law but under grace?" (6:15)

He undoubtedly encountered these challenges to grace in every synagogue between Jerusalem and Rome.

—6:1—

A rhetorical question is actually a statement merely disguised as a query and, therefore, does not expect an outright answer. But it is effective in debate because it makes a seemingly irrefutable statement and puts the opponent on the spot. Paul takes his opponents' rhetorical question, a challenge to the doctrine of grace, and puts it on display: "If sin brings grace, and lots of sin brings a lot more grace, shouldn't we sin as much as possible in order to keep grace flowing from heaven?" The opponents' response would naturally follow: "We know that can't be true; so the doctrine of grace must be false."

Paul's opponents have made a valid point. A depraved mind will certainly see grace from a twisted perspective. But Paul turns the attack to his advantage. His opponents have demonstrated all too clearly by their distorted point of view that God cannot allow those who receive His grace to remain in their depraved state of mind or they will mangle grace as Paul's detractors did. Therefore, believers must receive a new nature, a new mind.

—6:2–3—

Paul responds to the faulty notion with a strong rebuke: "May it never be!" That is, "May such a thing never occur!" He then put two more rhetorical questions before his readers, each containing a monumental Christian truth. The first question, "How shall we who died to sin still live in it?" highlights the fact that believers no longer serve their old master. We had been enslaved to sin because our old nature found it irresistible. But death has freed us from that bondage. How tragic it would be if an emancipated slave continued to suffer the pain of mistreatment and the degradation of servitude when he or she could run free!

Naturally, this begs the question, "How is it we died to sin when we are obviously very much alive?" Paul answers with a second rhetorical question: "Do you not know that all of us who have been baptized into Christ Jesus have been baptized into His death?" And this second question introduces a complex truth called "identification." According to this truth, all those who have placed their faith in Jesus Christ have been "baptized into" Him. The context makes it clear that this is not water baptism. This is a strong word picture that would have been familiar to the Roman believers, especially the Jews.

The word "baptize" is a transliteration of the Greek term *baptizō*, which means "to immerse, submerge." To be baptized into something is to be completely enveloped by it. Furthermore, the primary significance of baptism was identity. New converts to Judaism were baptized into the God's covenant with Abraham, so that they became identified with natural-born Jews and became heirs to all that God promised Abraham's Hebrew descendents.

When we place our trust in Jesus Christ for salvation from sin, we are said to be enveloped by Him in a spiritual sense. In a very real way, our identity becomes united with His, such that His experience becomes ours. He died and we died with Him. He rose from the dead to a new kind of life, and so shall we. By virtue of our identification with Jesus Christ, His death, and His resurrection, we have been emancipated from bondage to sin. Identity with Christ began with belief, but it has ongoing consequences.

This is a difficult concept because it's so abstract. But it's really not that much different from the truth we learned in Romans 3:21 – 5:21. We were identified with Jesus Christ when He suffered punishment on our behalf and He paid the legal penalty for sin in our place. God then credited His Son's righteousness to our moral accounts and we receive this grace through faith. But grace doesn't stop there.

Warren Weirsbe has created a chart that beautifully illustrates the continuing benefits of the grace we receive through faith in Jesus Christ.[4]

Romans 3:21–5:21	Romans 6–8
Substitution: He died for me	Identification: I died with Him
He died for my sins	He died unto sin
He paid sin's penalty	He broke sin's power
Justification: righteousness imputed (put to my account)	Sanctification: righteousness imparted (made a part of my life)
Saved by His death	Saved by His life

Identification allows the believer to partake of everything the Son of God enjoys. To help believers make the most of this gift, Paul first explains the intricacies of this vital Christian truth (6:4 – 10), outlines the significance of identification (6:11 – 12), and then concludes with an explanation of how to apply it (6:12). Three key terms to watch:

Know
Consider
Present

— 6:4 (Know Truth) —

Emancipation legally releases a person from involuntary bondage, but it doesn't guarantee that he or she will experience freedom. The person must first *know* that he or she has been released.

Paul's explanation of identification uses three conditional terms: "Therefore ... so that ... so [that] ..." The conjunction "therefore" (*oun*) is important because it indicates that the apostle's next statement is a logical continuation of what he has just written. In other words, the next sentence doesn't stand alone; it further explains the truth, "All of us who have been baptized into Christ Jesus have been baptized into death" (6:3). Therefore, "[because we have been baptized into death], we have been buried with Him through [the same] baptism [just mentioned] into death." The baptism of 6:4 is the same as that in 6:3—spiritual, not water.

I want to make this clear because some claim that grace and the promises of salvation are received through a pool of water and not through faith alone. Paul labored to establish the truth that circumcision—an important symbol of Jewish participation in God's covenant with Abraham—does not have the power to save anyone. Circumcision is a "notary seal" intended to verify the authenticity of one's faith. Remember that it was Abraham's faith that was credited to him as righteousness. Similarly, water baptism—an important symbol of Christian participation in God's new covenant through Christ—does not have the power to save anyone. Water baptism is a "notary seal" that verifies the authenticity of one's spiritual baptism into Christ.

The words and phrases of 6:4 are densely packed with meaning, so let me break the verse down this way:

"Therefore …"	As a logical consequence …
"we have been buried with Him …"	our experience is His experience …
"through baptism …"	through our identification with Him …
"into death …"	in that He was enveloped by death …
"so that as Christ was raised …"	so that, in the very same manner in which Christ was resurrected …
"through the glory of the Father …"	by the power of God the Father …
"so we too might …"	we would, potentially, …
"walk in newness of life."	experience the new kind of life Christ experienced and then conduct ourselves accordingly.

— **6:5–7** —

As a logical consequence of our identification with Christ in His death (His dying in our place), we will be identified with Him in His resurrection. This is true whether we know it or not. In eternity, we will be like Him. Our bodies will be like His; we will not be subject to pain, suffering, weakness, or temptation. However, in the meantime, while we live in these bodies in a fallen creation, this new kind of life is potentially ours. To experience it here and now, we must claim it (see 1 John 3:2–3).

"Body of sin" is an expression that Paul will explain in greater detail later. For now, we need only recognize that while the body is not inherently evil (as some claim), it is nonetheless the vehicle of our old sinful nature. It is not inherently sinful; however, it is a part of this fallen world and, therefore, subject to temptation and corruption. In a spiritual sense, we have died. Dead bodies don't respond to temptation. Dead bodies don't choose to do wrong. Temptation and sin have no power over corpses. And someday we will experience this truth in a physical sense. In the meantime, before we die physically and are raised to a new kind of life physically, we have the opportunity to experience this truth.

The first step toward experiencing this new, abundant Christ-life is "knowing this" (6:6). Knowing what? That "our old self was crucified with Him, in order that our body of sin might be done away with." In other words, we are under new management. We are subject to God's authority rather than that of sin, or the world, or any other ruler. We are no longer obligated to choose sin.

When I first began my years in the Marine Corps, I was subject to the authority of a drill instructor, perhaps the most intimidating, overpowering authority I have ever encountered. His objective: to break the wills of simple country boys and street-wise city slickers, to turn strong-willed boys into strong-hearted warriors. Drill instructors aren't known for their compassion. They tell you every move to make; when to eat, when to drink, when to sleep, when to wake up, and even when to relieve yourself. And the consequences for disobedience are extreme.

After basic training, I was told where to live and what job to do. And the Marine Corps didn't ask me if it was okay to ship me to the other side of the globe from my wife and to keep me there for sixteen months. The relationship was simple. They told me what to do and that I was obliged to do it. Then, I was honorably discharged, leaving me no longer under their authority.

Many years later, I waited to board a flight in Dallas-Fort Worth Airport and I heard a familiar sound echoing from my distant past. "YOU PEOPLE GET IN LINE. A STAIGHT LINE! DO YOU KNOW WHAT A STRAIGHT LINE IS? YOU STAND HERE. YOU THERE!" I'd know that sound anywhere! A pair of drill instructors prepared a bunch of raw recruits to board a plane for boot camp.

I watched all of this while standing to one side. After a few moments, one looked my way and I said, "How's it going, Gunny? Got all these wet-nosed kids in line?" He looked at me, flashed a grin, and said, "Yes, Sir." I had a great time with him. Why? Because he had no authority over me. He even said "Sir" to me! If he had tried to order me into line, I would have laughed out loud, done a quick about-face, and marched myself into a coffee shop! I don't have to obey Marine Corps drill instructors, or even generals for that matter. They no longer have control over me.

When we died with Christ, our bodies were relieved from submission to sin. We've been honorably discharged.

— 6:8–11 (Consider Truth) —

Once we know that God's gift is available, we must claim it. Paul continues his reasoning with another logical conjunction, "if" (*ei*). In this case, the "if" is conditional because what follows is only true for those who have believed and have therefore "died with Christ." If we have died with Christ, we believe we will also live with Him; that is, have the same kind of life He has. And this new kind of life can never end in death.

Jesus raised His friend Lazarus from the dead ... temporarily (John 11). Sometime later, Lazarus succumbed to disease or old age or disaster, and he died again. This is not the kind of resurrection Jesus experienced. He was raised to a new kind of life. His physical body not only awakened from death, it was transformed into a kind of body that was no longer subject to disease, disaster, or aging. It was no longer a body that the world could abuse. This will be true of us when our bodies have died and we are raised to this new kind of life.

That's a marvelous future we can anticipate with confident assurance. However, we don't have to wait. We can begin enjoying the benefits of this truth now. The death Christ died, He died on behalf of all (3:21–5:21); and the new kind of life He now lives, He lives "to God" (chs. 6–8). The resurrected life has God as both its source and its purpose. And to claim this gift, we must "consider" or "reckon" it to be true and then act on it. Paul, based on his authority as an agent of the good news, commands believers, "Consider yourselves to be dead to sin." Reckon it as true. Claim this truth as a reality. Count on it and live it out.

— 6:12–13 (Present Truth) —

Once we *know* about our emancipation from slavery and have *considered* ourselves to be freed from that old bondage, we must *present* ourselves to our new Master to enjoy the benefits of new life.

Slaves do the bidding of their master. They are the master's instruments, utilized by him to accomplish his desires. Before emancipation, we could not refuse sin's authority; but now we do not have to obey its commands. Rather than allowing our physical bodies to be instruments of sin's desire, "unrighteousness," we must now present our bodies to our new Master, God, to accomplish His desire, "righteousness."

The Greek word translated "instrument" frequently refers to weapons of war. We are no longer to present our bodies as weapons to be used by sin to accomplish evil ends, but to become foot soldiers in the interest of righteousness.

— 6:14 —

Paul concludes his point with a summary statement: "Sin shall not be master over you." Then he introduces his next point: "You are not under law but under grace." Because we have been freed from the bondage of sin, laws have no application. The purpose of the Law is to point out transgression; therefore, those who have no involvement in sin are not subject to laws.

I am certainly far from perfect; however, I have never been tempted to use illicit drugs. They have nothing to offer me, and if they suddenly ceased to exist, nothing about my life would be any different. So, if the laws concerning the sale and possession of heroin suddenly changed, I would not be affected in the least. Heroin has no place in my life, so laws restricting me from selling or using it are irrelevant. As far as I'm concerned, those statues may as well not exist. They have no meaning for me. In other words, I am not "under" those laws.

Imagine someone whose nature had been so completely transformed that he or she lost all desire for anything sinful. He or she would no longer be subject to laws — not only those concerning heroin, but all laws. That person could live the rest of his or her days as though laws, policemen, courts, and prisons didn't exist. Furthermore, that transformed spirit could live as though God had never defined which actions are sinful and which are not. Rules restricting his or her behavior would be irrelevant. This, according to Paul, is the potential of someone who is subject to the transforming power of grace.

Grace is not of this world. It is supernatural in origin and unfathomable to a depraved mind. So it should be no surprise that a newly emancipated spirit struggles to understand and apply something so foreign to its old nature.

I am told by those who studied under Lewis Sperry Chafer, the founder and first president of Dallas Theological Seminary, that he spent the last of his eighty-one years teaching systematic theology from a wheelchair. His favorite topic was grace. A mentor of mine who studied under Chafer told me that after a particularly moving lecture, the aged professor closed his Bible, rolled over to the door, and turned off the lights. The students never moved. Then he said, "I have spent all my life studying the grace of God and I am just now beginning to understand a little of it. And, gentlemen, it is magnificent."

The men who studied under Dr. Chafer and who later became mentors of mine were all models of grace. Every one. The winsome charm of grace has powerful, lasting influence on others. Tragically, the same can be said of legalism.

Application

The Best Life Now

Because grace is so foreign to the depraved mind, it is not easy for a newly restored mind to adjust. Nevertheless, the Holy Spirit will be faithful to use every circumstance and all experiences to transform the new believer from within. Eventually, when this physical life gives way to eternal life, we believers will be like Christ (1 John 3:2). Until then, we are works in progress.

While the Holy Spirit is able to do the work of transformation and will be faithful to complete the task (Phil. 1:6), we are invited to participate in that process. We have a genuine stake in determining the quality of life we enjoy here and now. Of course, the quality of life I am referring to has little to do with our physical circumstances. I am referring to authentic joy, intimacy with the Almighty, liberty from the compulsions of sin, and becoming like Christ. God will be faithful to accomplish in us what He wills, but the degree to which we participate either helps or hinders our progress.

Growing in grace begins with three specific changes in how we operate. This pattern will be repeated each time we encounter a new spiritual truth.

Know the truth (6:3–10). In this case, the truth of our new spiritual condition is that we are dead to sin. Before we believed in Christ, we were enslaved to evil. We did not possess the power to stop our own wrongdoing. Now, sin has only one weapon: deception. Satan wants you to think that compulsions to sin cannot be broken. But the truth stands. We are free!

Consider the truth (6:11). Once we encounter a new truth, we must discard our old manner of thinking and replace it with this new understanding. Often, that's not easy. We have been conditioned by the old pattern of thinking unconsciously to behave a certain way. Furthermore, we have become emotionally attached to our old manner of living—even when it's unpleasant. Habits are tough to break. Therefore, we must repeatedly and continually "consider" divine truth; that is, we must *decide* it is true.

Present our bodies to truth (6:12–13). Having decided something is true, we must change our behavior accordingly. Paul expresses this command in its most basic terms. Your mind controls your body, so take command and make your body operate in agreement with what you have accepted as true.

Imagine what it would be like if a billionaire were to inform you that for no other reason than kindness, he or she deposited one hundred million dollars into your checking account. Completely free. No strings attached. After taxes. I don't know how you would respond, but here's what I would do.

Know the truth. I would contact the president of my bank and verify that the funds are indeed credited to my account.

Consider the truth. I would take out my checkbook (yes, I still carry one!), make an entry in the register to reflect the deposit, and adjust my balance.

Present my body to the truth. After a substantial donation to my church and several favorite ministries, I would start writin' checks! I might struggle to accept the truth of my super-wealth, but I would make every effort to apply the necessary adjustments.

If you presently struggle with a particular repetitive or compulsive sin, you likely suffer from the delusion that you will never loosen its grip on you. I won't insult you by saying that transformation will be easy. It isn't. However, the truth is uncomplicated. If you are a believer, if you have accepted God's free gift of eternal life though faith in Jesus Christ, you have within you spiritual riches beyond your imagination. The power to overcome any evil lives within you. He is none other than God in the person of the Holy Spirit. Call on Him to help!

Knowing, considering, and presenting is not the entire solution to our problems, and I don't mean to oversimplify the process of spiritual growth. Deeply entrenched patterns of sin require much more attention than a simple accounting procedure. However, it is a necessary beginning.

So, don't wait. Begin now. It's never too late to start doing what is right.

Whose Slave Are You? (Romans 6:15–23)

15What then? Shall we sin because we are not under law but under grace? May it never be! 16Do you not know that when you present yourselves to someone *as* slaves for obedience, you are slaves of the one whom you obey, either of sin resulting in death, or of obedience resulting in righteousness? 17But thanks be to God that though you were slaves of sin, you became obedient from the heart to that form of teaching to which you were committed, 18and having been freed from sin, you became slaves of righteousness. 19I am speaking in human terms because of the weakness of your flesh. For just as you presented your members as slaves to impurity and to lawlessness, resulting in *further* lawlessness, so now present your members as slaves to righteousness, resulting in sanctification. [20]For when you were slaves of sin, you were free in regard to righteousness. [21]Therefore what benefit were you then deriving from the things of which you are now ashamed? For the outcome of those things is death. [22]But now having been freed from sin and enslaved to God, you derive your benefit, resulting in sanctification, and the outcome, eternal life. [23]For the wages of sin is death, but the free gift of God is eternal life in Christ Jesus our Lord.

One of my mentors, Ray Stedman, ministered in the San Francisco area of California, which has always been an interesting place. This was especially true during the sixties and seventies. One year, J. Vernon McGee invited him to preach a series of messages at the Church of the Open Door in Los Angeles, which Ray gladly did. During a break one evening, he strolled down Hope Street, which reminded him a lot of his own mission field up north. He didn't go very far before encountering one of the area's more colorful residents; an eccentric man with long, tangled hair, a scraggly beard, and filthy clothes walked toward him wearing a sandwich board. Written on the front in bold letters—no doubt by the man himself—were the words, "I am a slave for Jesus Christ." The scruffy prophet held Ray's eyes in a steady gaze until he passed by, and as he continued up the sidewalk, Ray turned to read the backside of the sandwich board. It read, "Whose slave are you?"

A good question asked by a strange example! We all serve something; it's just a matter of what.

Some are slaves of their work. These servants of busyness and achievement can't shut down their laptops for more than a couple of hours at a time and their electronic devices are all but surgically implanted in their hands. They take working vacations to appease neglected loved ones and miserly hoard days off they never intend to take. A balanced life always lies just beyond the current project deadline.

Some are slaves to things, possessions, temporal stuff. Driven by the fantasy that contentment can be found in the having of things, they cannot stop acquiring long enough to enjoy what they already own, which prompts the question, "How much is enough?" H. L. Hunt, the billionaire oil tycoon, is credited with the most honest reply I've heard to date: "Money is just a way of keeping score."

Perhaps more than ever, people are enslaved to relationships. They magically mutate into whatever pleasing shape will gain them the approval of another. They cycle between self-acceptance and self-loathing, depending upon the affirmation or criticism they receive. They eagerly sacrifice themselves and, ironically, those they love to avoid the most dreadful condition of all: aloneness.

Perhaps the most pathetic and increasingly common slaves are those who are enslaved to the god of self. Psychologists call them narcissists. The name comes from a figure in Roman mythology named Narcissus, who fell in love with his own reflection in a stream. When he tried to kiss the object of his love, his lips disturbed the water and his image ran away, which left him heartbroken. He dared not drink from the stream for fear of losing his lover forever. Eventually, the slave of self-love died of thirst.

Narcissists serve themselves, even when they appear to be selfless, and they relentlessly demand the time, attention, admiration, devotion, and nurturing of others. But this, like the other forms of slavery, only leads to greater emptiness.

We all serve something; it's just a matter of what.

—6:15–16—

Paul concluded his response to the question, "Are we to continue in sin so that grace may increase?" (6:1), with the statement, "Sin shall not be master over you, for you are not under law but under grace" (6:14). In other words, because believers can now choose not to sin, they have the freedom to rise above the law. This prompts a second rhetorical question—again, one Paul likely heard often in response to the gospel: "Shall we sin because we are not under law but under grace?"

Paul again responds emotionally, saying in effect: "May such a thing never occur!" He then demonstrates the absurdity of the question, beginning with a rhetorical question of his own. (Remember, a rhetorical question is really a statement in the form of a query.) "Do you not know that when you present yourselves to someone as slaves for obedience, you are slaves of the one whom you obey, either of sin resulting in death, or of obedience resulting in righteousness?" The apostle reminds his readers that a man is a slave to the one he commits himself to obey. And to be a slave of something is to become an instrument in serving its interests (6:12–13). Because grace has freed us, we now have a choice between two masters. The old master, "sin," is dedicated to the destruction of those who serve it. The new master, "obedience," seeks righteousness, those things that please God and give life to those who serve Him.

The ancient Romans were well known for their slavery, which took two forms. The more familiar kind of slavery involved capturing an enemy, destroying anything that might tempt him to return home, and then transporting him to Rome for sale on the auction block. But an older, more common type of slavery was "voluntary indenture." Impoverished people could offer themselves as slaves to someone in order to have food to eat and a place to live. In other words, people willingly accepted slavery in order to meet their basic needs.

In the American South after the Civil War, many freed slaves had no other choice but to become "sharecroppers," which gave them land and livelihood, but required them to "share" most of their produce with the landowner. Of course, this was merely servitude with a gentler, kinder name. Nevertheless, no one chose a cruel master except as a last resort.

Paul asks, in effect, "Why would you choose a master whose dedicated purpose is to keep you enslaved and ultimately kill you? That's like an emancipated slave choosing to help his old master reinforce his chains and build a gallows! Why would anyone willingly serve such a cruel master?"

We have basic needs we must have met. And we have a choice between two masters. To whom will we go? Whose interests will we serve? One promises life; the other, death.

Serve sin? What an absurd thought!

—6:17–18—

This prompts Paul to break out into a spontaneous doxology: "Thanks be to God!" The gospel has present, ongoing, and eternal implications. Eternal life begins sometime in our future, after this life has ended. But something happens immediately when a person receives the grace of God through faith. He or she is instantly given a new heart, a new nature that hates sin and desires to obey its new master: righteousness.

—6:19—

As a pastor, I can appreciate Paul's parenthetical comment. A good illustration has the power to simplify and clarify difficult concepts. Charles Spurgeon likened a great sermon to a cathedral, which would be dark inside were it not for the windows of illustration. Illustrations allow light to fill the space so everyone can see clearly. However, a particularly good illustration can take on a life of its own and become a distraction. Preachers have to be careful not to turn an analogy into an allegory. While the illustration of slavery is powerful, it is flawed in one important respect. The truth Paul labors to teach is really a paradox. Slavery to God is the greatest freedom a human can ever know.

When God created Adam and Eve, they perfectly bore their Creator's image. They lived in perfect harmony with their created purpose, which was to live in limitless communion with Him, to enjoy uninhibited intimacy with one another, and to rule over the rest of creation as His vice-regents. Never was humankind so free as when they lived in harmony with their created purpose, or as Paul chooses to put it, "as slaves to righteousness."

When we "serve righteousness," we not only please God, we do what is best for ourselves. That's how the Lord created the universe to work before it was corrupted through disobedience. But humanity exchanged truth for a lie and looked to sin rather than their Creator to meet their basic needs. That decision only perpetuated sin and intensified the accompanying bondage. This is the downward cycle of sin.

The grace of God changed all of that. Christ's sacrificial death creates the potential for us to recapture some of the innocence and freedom of Eden. Just as service to sin binds us closer to sin, service to righteousness frees us to live in harmony with our created purpose, which is to live in limitless communion with God, enjoy uninhibited intimacy with one another, and rule over the rest of creation as His vice-regents. Paul called this *hagiasmos*, which is commonly translated "sanctification, holiness, consecration, or purity." For Paul, sanctification is both a state of being and a process. While it appears only twice in his letter (6:19, 22), it is nevertheless the central theme of this larger section (Romans 6–8).

— **6:20-22** —

Again, Paul clarifies the believer's choice. Sin and righteousness are mutually exclusive. In the words of Jesus, "No one can serve two masters; for either he will hate the one and love the other, or he will be devoted to one and despise the other" (Matt. 6:24). Moreover, human nature abhors a vacuum. God created humanity with certain needs. In the beginning, those physical, emotional, and spiritual needs were filled as humankind enjoyed peace with God. After the Fall, we looked to sin instead.

This leads the apostle to ask another rhetorical question, not as a clever strategy of debate, but to prompt the reader to look within. He asks, in effect, "When you were trying to meet those God-given needs by pursuing sin, what did you gain?"

For centuries, people have turned to mind-altering drugs for a variety of reasons, but the most basic desire is to feel good rather than bad. They usually find that the payoff is immediate and immensely satisfying ... in the short term. Medical experts tell us that these drugs have a double impact in the long term: they increase the user's need for the drug while decreasing his or her body's response. In other words, the drug gradually creates a greater need for more, and it takes larger and larger doses to achieve the same satisfying effect.

The same is true of sin. Sin is usually the result of someone trying to fill a legitimate, God-given need in an illegitimate way. Paul reminds his readers that once we have been freed from bondage to sin, we still have needs that must be filled. And we will look to something to fill them. As I stated before, we all serve something; it's just a matter of what.

The believer, having been freed from bondage to sin—released from his or her addiction to sin, as it were—may now look to the Creator for fulfillment. While the pull of sin is down, the cycle of sanctification draws the believer closer to God. Increasing dependence on the Lord provides meaningful satisfaction and, ironically, greater freedom. And rather than leading to death, slavery to God ultimately leads to eternal life.

Who wouldn't want that?

—6:23—

Paul masterfully concludes his answer to the charge that grace encourages sin with a succinct couplet. Take note of the contrast:

The wages		The free gift
of sin	BUT	of God
is death,		is eternal life

This verse is commonly used to explain the gospel to those who have yet to believe, but Paul writes it to encourage believers in sanctification. And in this concluding statement, he introduces a new concept, one that he will take great care to explain in the next chapter.

In chapter 6, Paul has stated that those who place their trust in Jesus Christ and receive God's grace through faith are "baptized into" Him. Believers are therefore identified with Him so that His experiences become our experiences, His blessings become our blessings, and His power becomes our power. We have none of the above on our own. We have everything by virtue of our being "in Christ." We are "dead to sin, but alive to God *in Christ*" (6:11). Moreover, we receive eternal life by being "in Christ" (6:23).

This "in Christ" concept becomes the key to understanding everything Paul tells his readers in the following chapters. The believer's life derives from being in Christ, his or her joy must be found in Christ, his or her success depends on resting in Christ, and we have fellowship with others who are in Christ.

As we will see, our being "in Christ" provides the opportunity to escape the downward drag of sin and to enjoy freedom as we never thought possible. However, it's no guarantee that we will experience that kind of joy in this lifetime. Like emancipation, we must "know" (understand its truth), "consider" (claim its truth), and "present" (apply its truth). Unfortunately, our old master refuses to release its grip. The emancipation proclamation has gone out; nevertheless a war rages around us and within us. If you are a believer in the Lord Jesus Christ, you have a daily question to answer, and your response will lead either to life or death. Whose slave are you?

Application

Choose Your Master

Paul boldly declares that we are no longer compelled to serve sin or accomplish the purposes of unrighteousness (6:15–21). We may freely choose to obey sin and then reap its sorrowful consequences, or we may freely choose to obey Christ and then share in His joy (6:20–23).

As I reflect on Paul's words and review my years in pastoral ministry, I find that much of my time is spent combating one of two problems.

First, *it is possible to be a slave to something and think you are free.* This is the

"IN CHRIST" IN ROMANS

The phrase, "in Christ," is deeply meaningful for Paul and appears no less than eighty-four times in his letters, thirteen times in his letter to the Romans.

Rom 3:24	… being justified as a gift by His grace through the redemption which is in Christ Jesus;
Rom 6:11	Even so consider yourselves to be dead to sin, but alive to God in Christ Jesus.
Rom 6:23	For the wages of sin is death, but the free gift of God is eternal life in Christ Jesus our Lord.
Rom 8:1	Therefore there is now no condemnation for those who are in Christ Jesus.
Rom 8:2	For the law of the Spirit of life in Christ Jesus has set you free from the law of sin and of death.
Rom 8:39	… nor height, nor depth, nor any other created thing, will be able to separate us from the love of God, which is in Christ Jesus our Lord.
Rom 9:1	I am telling the truth in Christ, I am not lying, my conscience testifies with me in the Holy Spirit,
Rom 12:5	… so we, who are many, are one body in Christ, and individually members one of another.
Rom 15:17	Therefore in Christ Jesus I have found reason for boasting in things pertaining to God.
Rom 16:3	Greet Prisca and Aquila, my fellow workers in Christ Jesus,
Rom 16:7	Greet Andronicus and Junias, my kinsmen and my fellow prisoners, who are outstanding among the apostles, who also were in Christ before me.
Rom 16:9	Greet Urbanus, our fellow worker in Christ, and Stachys my beloved.
Rom 16:10	Greet Apelles, the approved in Christ. Greet those who are of the household of Aristobulus.

predicament of the lost. They slavishly serve something they think will bring them fulfillment or eliminate their problems. Money, career, sex, relationships, adventure, power, notoriety, education, achievement, even addictions … the idols of this world are legion. I see people sacrifice to keep their god alive and fear what life will be if—or when—the object of their hope passes away. And I stand amazed at their inability to comprehend the extent of their slavery, all the while trying to convince themselves and others that life is good just the way it is. Moreover, they refuse to heed the good news for fear that submission to Christ will take away their freedom!

Second, *it is possible to be free and think you are enslaved*. This second problem is almost as tragic as the first. Counseling offices around the world are filled with Christians who struggle to accept the fact that they no longer must serve imaginary gods. They remain shackled to compulsions, hiding in shame, unaware that they now worship a God who doesn't demand but empowers. They have peace with God, who does not condemn His children but who longs to see them victorious over sin.

The remedy for both problems is the same: *truth*.

On the one hand, unbelievers need to know that "the wages of sin is death, but the free gift of God is eternal life in Christ Jesus our Lord" (6:23). The "freedom" they experience is an illusion designed to draw their attention away from the fact that sin is robbing them of everything they value and will eventually drag them into eternal torment.

Believers, on the other hand, must learn to embrace their freedom and recognize temptation for what it is. Each opportunity to sin is an invitation to submit our bodies to something. Temptation asks the following question: "To which master will you submit your body for the next few moments: your compulsion, which always leaves you feeling emptier than before, or Christ, who always affirms your value as a child of God?"

Frankly, I have found that simply *not* doing something wrong when tempted is not enough. I need something else to which I can submit my body. Here is a four-step process that I find helpful when tempted to do wrong:

1. *Flee temptation*; that is, change your circumstances. Physically move from where you are and quickly go somewhere different, even if it's just for a few minutes.
2. *Do something that brings honor to God as an alternative*. Prayer is good, but I suggest adding something more tangible. Systematically answer the urge to sin with a godly activity.
3. Thank God for providing the freedom to choose Him over wrongdoing and ask Him for encouragement. Spiritual warfare is exhausting!

4. Try to discern what triggered the temptation and take practical steps to steer clear of the same situation.

Portrait of a Struggling Christian (Romans 7:1–25)

---

[1]Or do you not know, brethren (for I am speaking to those who know the law), that the law has jurisdiction over a person as long as he lives? [2]For the married woman is bound by law to her husband while he is living; but if her husband dies, she is released from the law concerning the husband. [3]So then, if while her husband is living she is joined to another man, she shall be called an adulteress; but if her husband dies, she is free from the law, so that she is not an adulteress though she is joined to another man. [4]Therefore, my brethren, you also were made to die to the Law through the body of Christ, so that you might be joined to another, to Him who was raised from the dead, in order that we might bear fruit for God. [5]For while we were in the flesh, the sinful passions, which were *aroused* by the Law, were at work in the members of our body to bear fruit for death. [6]But now we have been released from the Law, having died to that by which we were bound, so that we serve in newness of the Spirit and not in oldness of the letter. [7]What shall we say then? Is the Law sin? May it never be! On the contrary, I would not have come to know sin except through the Law; for I would not have known about coveting if the Law had not said, "You shall not covet." [8]But sin, taking opportunity through the commandment, produced in me coveting of every kind; for apart from the Law sin is dead. [9]I was once alive apart from the Law; but when the commandment came, sin became alive and I died; [10]and this commandment, which was to result in life, proved to result in death for me; [11]for sin, taking an opportunity through the commandment, deceived me and through it killed me. [12]So then, the Law is holy, and the commandment is holy and righteous and good. [13]Therefore did that which is good become *a cause of* death for me? May it never be! Rather it was sin, in order that it might be shown to be sin by effecting my death through that which is good, so that through the commandment sin would become utterly sinful. [14]For we know that the Law is spiritual, but I am of flesh, sold into bondage to sin. [15]For what I am doing, I do not understand; for I am not practicing what I *would* like to *do*, but I am doing the very thing I hate. [16]But if I do the very thing I do not want *to do*, I agree with the Law, *confessing* that the Law is good. [17]So now, no longer am I the one doing it, but sin which dwells in me. [18]For I know that nothing good dwells in me, that is, in my flesh; for the willing is present in me, but the doing of the good is not. [19]For the good

that I want, I do not do, but I practice the very evil that I do not want. [20]But if I am doing the very thing I do not want, I am no longer the one doing it, but sin which dwells in me.

[21]I find then the principle that evil is present in me, the one who wants to do good. [22]For I joyfully concur with the law of God in the inner man, [23]but I see a different law in the members of my body, waging war against the law of my mind and making me a prisoner of the law of sin which is in my members. [24]Wretched man that I am! Who will set me free from the body of this death? [25]Thanks be to God through Jesus Christ our Lord! So then, on the one hand I myself with my mind am serving the law of God, but on the other, with my flesh the law of sin.

As portrait painters go, few can match the realism of Dimitri Vail. His choice of colors and shading, his attention to minute details, even the texture of his brush strokes gave his paintings such a literal quality you weren't quite sure it wasn't a photograph. I visited his gallery more than once, many years ago. It was in an old part of Dallas. Walking down the long, narrow corridor where the portraits hung was like stepping back in time for a visit with Hollywood's luminaries. Each frame was labeled with a small brass engraving of the subject's name, as if anyone needed them.

Bill Cosby grinned at me with that characteristic tight-lipped smile of his. I saw comedians, Rowan and Martin hanging right next to Martin and Lewis. There was Benny Goodman with his clarinet, which he played with such ease, alongside Jack Benny with his violin, which made the most torturous sounds imaginable. John Wayne, James Dean, Red Buttons, Ed Sullivan, Frank Sinatra, and Sophie Tucker. They were all there along with a few presidents, astronauts, and world-class athletes. At the end of the long row of the world's brightest, boldest, and most beautiful people hung a dimly lit portrait of a somber, almost sad figure. The frame was smaller and more rugged than the others, and it didn't bear the name of the subject. So I asked the attendant to come over and tell me about the painting.

"Who is this?" I asked.

She smiled knowingly and said, "I'm asked that question a lot. This is a self-portrait of the artist. He painted it rather recently, during a period of intense personal struggle. He chose to put it here. It isn't for sale."

I admit to being surprised. I supposed I expected that someone who ran with people of this caliber—celebrities, popular heroes, and politicians—would have been a perpetual-motion machine of joy and excitement. Instead, he was a man like many I've known, struggling with life.

As far as we know, the apostle Paul never held an artist's brush. Nevertheless, his portrait of humanity, done in pen and ink, hangs in the gallery of his letter to the

Romans. The first frame bears the name "Lost Person," and it's bluntly accurate. His is a picture of depravity, emptiness, and pride. The second frame holds the image of a grateful figure named "Justified Sinner." Newly freed from the death grip of sin, this person can barely contain his joy. The next frame is encouraging because it captures the exuberance of one "Victorious Believer." He has discovered that, in reality, eternal life doesn't begin after death; it begins the moment one believes in Christ.

At the end of the corridor, a dark picture hangs. The subject is a sad, exhausted, defeated man. Who is this, you ask? It's a self-portrait of the artist. It's Paul. If you dust off the brass nameplate, you'll see the name, written in his own hand: "Wretched Man."

Romans 7 is Paul's self-portrait, in which he uses the first person singular pronoun, "I," almost thirty times. Near the end of his verbal self-portrait, he exclaims, "Wretched man that I am!" The term "wretched" is translated from a Greek word that means "suffering, afflicted, miserable."

In Texas, we have a slang term for squeezing water out of wet clothing. You "wrench" the water out of something when you roll the article up, hold it at either end, and twist in opposite directions. That's the idea behind "wretched." Paul described himself as feeling like something had "wrenched" the life out of him. But why? How could this be? Obviously the portraits form a progression, beginning with "Lost" and rising to "Victorious." Why, after escaping the tyranny of sin, does the next portrait depict a suffering, afflicted, miserable man?

To find the answer, we must first understand the relationship between the believer and rules governing conduct, or "law."

—**7:1–4**—

Paul had earlier made the provocative statement that the believer is "not under law but under grace" (6:14). He now returns to explain how this could be true, first by way of a familiar illustration using civil law.

Paul proposes a hypothetical scenario for his readers to consider. In that scenario, a marriage between a man and a woman is apparently strained by her desire to be with another. But the law of marriage forbids her to leave her first husband to be married to someone else; this law would label her guilty of adultery. However, should her mate die, she will be released from her obligation to the law and can freely marry someone else. "Therefore"—that is, by the same reasoning—the believer's obligation to the Law of Moses has been terminated by death.

Paul's illustration involves three elements: A husband, a wife, and the law that regulates their behavior. Many make the mistake of casting the Law in the role of the husband, suggesting that the Law of Moses is like an autocratic, abusing mate who finally dies to the great relief of the surviving partner! But take note of who dies in Paul's application. He didn't state that the Law dies. It's still very much alive and active, fulfilling its purpose in God's redemptive plan. The *believer* dies, and with him, his marital obligations to sin (6:2, 18, 22). This becomes clear as Paul concludes his point in 7:6: "But now we have been released from the Law, having died to that by which we were bound." We were formerly bound to sin.

A relationship between the believer and the Law exists after his or her death "in Christ," but it's a very different relationship.

—7:5–6—

God gave the Law to accomplish two objectives. First, the Law exposes our *sins*. God gave His Law to confront us with our sin so that we might repent and come to Him in faith. (We learned this truth during our study of 5:12–13.) Second, the Law exposes our *sinfulness*. The Law rouses our rebellious nature into action, which demonstrates our inability to help ourselves and proves our need for God to change our hearts.

Years ago, one of the first high-rise hotels to open in Galveston, Texas, sat directly above the Gulf; it was so close to the water, in fact, that the owners worried that people would want to drop their fishing lines into the water from the guest room balconies. The high winds, the large lead sinkers, and the first story glass windows were certain to be a bad combination. Thus, the management placed a sign in each room facing the ocean:

ABSOLUTELY NO FISHING FROM THE BALCONY

What happened? You guessed it. Guests in the first story restaurant dined to the frequent smack of lead weights against the plate glass windows. Sometimes the glass literally cracked. Finally, the people managing the hotel realized their error and made a wise decision: they removed all the signs in the guest rooms.

Problem solved! No one ever fished from their balconies again.

Paul gives this rebellious nature a name. He calls it "the flesh," and his use of the term is unlike any other writer in the Bible. Throughout the New Testament, "flesh" is often used figuratively of humanity's material aspect, as opposed to our souls or spirits. Jesus once said that the flesh is weak (Matt. 26:41), but no one before Paul called it sinful or evil.[5]

Paul uses the term "flesh" symbolically to represent humanity it its fallen state. The flesh is programmed to think like the world system, which is a perverted version of God's original created order, and it continues to oppose His will. As the fallen world is opposed to grace, so the flesh is opposed to the Holy Spirit. And to be "in the flesh" is to be thinking and acting in concert with the fallen, depraved world as Paul described it in 1:18–32.

"But now," Paul declares, we have been released from our legal obligation to carry out the objectives of sin. Furthermore, our relationship with the Law has changed because we have a new nature that isn't opposed to the Law. Paul called this new nature "Spirit," with a capital "S," because it is God's Spirit whom we have received. Instead of living in harmony with the Law by studying it and following every letter (which we were powerless to do anyway), we allow the Spirit of God to live through us, who cannot disobey.

One poet has expressed the change this way:

A rigid master was the Law,
Demanding brick, denying straw;
But when with gospel-tongue it sings,
It bids me fly, and gives me wings.[6]

THE WORLD ACCORDING TO PLATO

Around 400 BC, a student of Socrates named Plato described the universe in terms that have influenced Western philosophy, science, and religion for millennia. In fact, much of Christian theology has been unwittingly influenced by the teaching of Plato, usually with dreadful consequences.

Plato divided the universe into two realms. The realm of "idea" (or "forms") consisted of all things theoretical. This intangible realm is perfect, orderly, morally pure, and eternal. It is the dwelling of *theos* ("god"), which is not a person as much as impersonal, the origin of reason and order. The realm of "materials" (or "substance"), by contrast, is the physical, material world we inhabit. It is a flawed, inferior representation of the far superior realm of idea.

In the realm of idea, for example, the concept "chair" is expressed in the material realm in various ways. There are dining room chairs, desk chairs, rocking chairs, and even reclining chairs. They are different, yet they all embody an intangible quality, or idea, that defines each of these items as a chair. However, these material representations are flawed. Unlike the incorruptible, eternal chair idea, they can be destroyed or altered or contaminated. Therefore, they are inferior; each material chair is a mere shadow of the real chair, which resides in the realm of idea.

This model of the universe became the source of endless religious and philosophical systems. Most of them saw people as fragments of pure idea, "spirits," trapped in corrupt material bodies of flesh. While the spirit of a person is pure and incorruptibly good, the body is a defiled prison, which is inherently bad.

Paul was familiar with Greek philosophy, but he rejected Plato's universe in favor of the Old Testament. Therefore, we must be careful to interpret "Spirit" and "flesh" as Paul intended, not as our culture, influenced by Greek philosophy, subtly suggests.

—7:7–13—

Paul probably feels his Jewish readers might misunderstand him at this point. His passionate tone might lead some to think he considers the Law evil or that grace opposes the Law. Others may have misinterpreted his illustrations to mean that sin and the Law are synonymous. So, he addresses the question directly: "Is the Law sinful?"

Again, the apostle responds emotionally: "May it never be!" Then, as always, he offers a thorough clarification. The Law is good for its intended purpose, which is to call us into account for sin and to expose the sinfulness of our "flesh." A modern-day illustration of Paul's clarification may help.

Not long ago, most people didn't find out about their cancer until it was too late. The first symptoms usually led to bad news from the doctor. Then someone invented the MRI, a marvelous machine that quickly and accurately probes the patient's flesh and yields a detailed image of his or her body. A trained eye can then examine the image and locate cancerous tumors long before the patient presents any symptoms. If the MRI leads to a diagnosis of cancer, the patient would be foolish to blame the machine for his illness. If anything, he should be thankful that his problem was discovered early enough to be treated.

In essence, Paul said, "I did not know that I was dying from the disease of sin until the Law revealed my terminal condition. Furthermore, the Law showed me that I loved my disease and that I would do anything to keep it. I was like a living dead man! By pointing out my problem, the Law demonstrated that I was living under a death sentence."

The Law is God's diagnostic tool. Its purpose is to expose the disease of sin and to confront us with the prognosis: the disease is deadly if not treated, but it's completely curable. Does the Law cause death? No more than the MRI causes cancer.

—7:14–16—

Paul introduced the concept of "the flesh" earlier, declaring it to be the opposite of Spirit. But he needs to explain how it continues to impact a believer, especially as the interactions become more complex. Before someone believes, the flesh serves sin and feels the condemnation of Law. Even if he or she wanted to obey the law consistently, any endeavor would soon end in failure. Once someone has received God's grace though faith, the Holy Spirit takes up residence in that believer. And so begins the internal struggle. The flesh continues to serve sin, while the Spirit serves righteousness. "For what I am doing, I do not understand; for I am not practicing what I would like to do, but I am doing the very thing I hate. But if I do the very thing I do not want to do, I agree with the Law, confessing that the Law is good" (7:15 – 16).

— 7:17 – 23 —

Paul describes the fleshly pull toward sin as the "dwelling-within-me sin." While he received a new nature when he believed in Jesus Christ, his body seems to have a mind of its own. It's as though he were conjoined to a person who loves the very things he hates most. And the same is true for every believer. Every Christian receives a new nature, one that wants nothing more than to behave as Jesus Christ behaves. Meanwhile the flesh, the old human nature, wants life to continue as it was. Here's part of the battle's description:

> So now, no longer am I the one doing it [what I don't want to do], but sin which dwells in me … nothing good dwells in me … for the willing is present in me, but the doing of the good is not. For the good that I want, I do not do, but I practice the very evil that I do not want … I joyfully concur with the law of God in the inner man, but I see a different law in the members of my body, waging war against the law of my mind and making me a prisoner of the law of sin which is in my members. (7:17 – 23)

Let me draw again upon the heroin analogy. Most experts agree that cold-turkey withdrawal from heroin addiction is one of the most excruciating ordeals a person can endure. Bone and muscle pain, insomnia, diarrhea, vomiting, and shock-like symptoms usually peak two or three days after the last dose, and it usually takes more than a week to subside. The physical anguish would be enough without the psychological trauma the addict suffers. Yet, even after enduring the torment of withdrawal and moving beyond physical dependence on the drug, many return to using it. The problems that encouraged the addict to escape into heroin are still present, and the craving for relief becomes too much to bear alone.

Anyone who has experienced physical dependence on anything will affirm that the craving is never far away. Even chronic smokers who have kicked the habit tell me that, years later, they sometimes long to enjoy a cigarette after a good meal. That's why drug treatment experts are unanimous in their opinion. Treating the body to overcome physical dependence is only a beginning. The key to lifelong sobriety lies in treating the mind, which is itself a lifelong endeavor. The addict is never really "cured." The addiction will always be a part of their lives. However, addicts can remain "in recovery" forever.

All of us are chronically addicted to sin. Long after we are saved, our bodies crave that which gave us short-term pleasure and caused long-term anguish. And the pull to indulge the craving for sin will always be a part of our lives ... at least until we are freed from "the body of this death" (v. 24). As for the present? "Wretched man that I am!"

—7:24–25—

Paul's description of his personal struggle with the old nature paints a bleak picture of the future for the average Christian, doesn't it? I readily admit that I am no Paul, so if he felt defeated, what hope is there for me?

Paul used the word "wretched" to describe himself. We don't use that word much in modern language, but I can think of no one word to replace it. So let me draw a word picture. Imagine a boxer after a fifteen-round pummeling. With months of training, hype, and dreams of championship glory down the drain, he stands exhausted, demoralized, barely able to see through the swelling around his eyes, and barely able to breathe with a couple of ribs fractured. And to make matters worse, he must take his place in the middle of the ring to hear his defeat announced to the crowd.

The fight Paul has described has left him wretched. Unable to defeat his flesh by means of his flesh—that is, by his own ability—he cries out for help. What, other than death, can free him from a body that craves sin more powerfully than his mind craves righteousness? Who will rescue him from his misery?

The answer comes quickly: "God—through Jesus Christ our Lord."

Just before I left Dimitri Vail's gallery in Dallas, the attendant said, "Our hope is that Mr. Vail will paint another portrait of himself on a better day." I don't know if he ever did. Fortunately, Paul didn't stop painting with chapter 7. His best work was yet to come. And because his hope is our hope, we can anticipate the same glorious future with confident assurance. Just wait and see.

Application

Chasing Rainbows, Self-Improvement, and Other Futile Pursuits

Once a believer has died to sin, "in Christ" his or her relationship with the Law is forever changed. The new covenant (Jer. 31:31–33) gives us a new rule of life: the Holy Spirit (7:1–6). God gave the Law to humanity to confront our unrighteousness and to demonstrate our need for salvation. Once a person abandons his or her futile attempt to keep the Law and receives God's grace through faith in Jesus Christ, the Law has served its purpose (7:7–13). The believer's relationship with the Law is then severed.

So, what is our goal in life now that we are saved? Is it not to please God by keeping the Law? Are we not to become like Christ, who is morally perfect? Shouldn't we repay God's kindness by pursuing good deeds and eradicating sin from our lives? Now that we are saved from condemnation by the grace of God, are we to sanctify ourselves through fasting, praying, studying Scripture, tithing, and the other spiritual disciplines?

If Paul's self-portrait teaches us anything, it's that self-improvement carried out in the energy of the flesh is a vain pursuit (7:14–25). You can push yourself to fatigue trying hard to be like Christ, but you will have an easier time catching rainbows. Some teachers and preachers acknowledge the impossibility of achieving the perfection of God, but nonetheless find value in aiming high. Others lower the standard of perfection to bring it within easier reach and then claim victory over sin. Most people simply work themselves into a wretched exhaustion and then collapse—sometimes with destructive force.

But God never demands perfection. (Read that again—aloud!) Untainted morality vanished with Eden. No, we are not saved by grace and then sanctified by our own labors. The work of grace is not half done. The point of Paul's miserable self-portrait in 7:13–25 is to demonstrate that humanity can no more purify itself of sin after salvation than before. Only God can purify a soul.

So, what is our duty now as believers saved by grace? Our primary purpose is to know Jesus Christ personally with ever-deepening intimacy (Phil. 3:8–11). If we read Scripture, pray, meditate, journal, or fast, let us do it for the sole purpose of knowing His mind. If we worship, serve, partake of communion, or spend time in the company of believers, let us learn about Him through His transforming work in others. If we feed the poor, defend the weak, comfort the lonely, or proclaim the gospel to a broken and needy world, let our walking in His sandals give us firsthand knowledge of His character. Let every trial or triumph bring us closer to knowing Christ's nature and to understanding His purposes.

The spiritual disciplines are not a means to holiness; they are a means of knowing Christ. As we engage in personal piety, have fellowship with other believers, and engage the world at large in the name of Christ—as we come to know Him more intimately—the Holy Spirit will do what only He can do: make us more like our Savior. As the moon reflects the light of the sun, yet has no light of its own, so we will shine with God's radiance as we live in proximity to His Son.

Now, *that* is a worthy pursuit.

Let's Talk About Our Walk (Romans 8:1–17)

[1]Therefore there is now no condemnation for those who are in Christ Jesus. [2]For the law of the Spirit of life in Christ Jesus has set you free from the law of sin and of death. [3]For what the Law could not do, weak as it was through the flesh, God *did*: sending His own Son in the likeness of sinful flesh and *as an offering* for sin, He condemned sin in the flesh, [4]so that the requirement of the Law might be fulfilled in us, who do not walk according to the flesh but according to the Spirit. [5]For those who are according to the flesh set their minds on the things of the flesh, but those who are according to the Spirit, the things of the Spirit. [6]For the mind set on the flesh is death, but the mind set on the Spirit is life and peace, [7]because the mind set on the flesh is hostile toward God; for it does not subject itself to the law of God, for it is not even able *to do so*, [8]and those who are in the flesh cannot please God.

[9]However, you are not in the flesh but in the Spirit, if indeed the Spirit of God dwells in you. But if anyone does not have the Spirit of Christ, he does not belong to Him. [10]If Christ is in you, though the body is dead because of sin, yet the spirit is alive because of righteousness. [11]But if the Spirit of Him who raised Jesus from the dead dwells in you, He who raised Christ Jesus from the dead will also give life to your mortal bodies through His Spirit who dwells in you.

[12]So then, brethren, we are under obligation, not to the flesh, to live according to the flesh — [13]for if you are living according to the flesh, you must die; but if by the Spirit you are putting to death the deeds of the body, you will live. [14]For all who are being led by the Spirit of God, these are sons of God. [15]For you have not received a spirit of slavery leading to fear again, but you have received a spirit of adoption as sons by which we cry out, "Abba! Father!" [16]The Spirit Himself testifies with our spirit that we are children of God, [17]and if children, heirs also, heirs of God and fellow heirs with Christ, if indeed we suffer with *Him* so that we may also be glorified with *Him*.

The drive from West Texas to Colorado is one of extremes, especially in the heat of summer. I've done it without air conditioning and I can only imagine what it would have been like on horseback. The journey starts in barren, dusty flatland that seems to go on forever. Endless hot miles pass beneath you as you travel up the Panhandle and, after monotonous hours, you begin to wonder if you'll ever cross the State line. Eventually, you do pass through the cleverly named town of Texline, Texas, into New Mexico to join the old Santa Fe Trail, now Interstate 25. Much of that terrain remains flat, dusty, and *hot*. Did I mention how oppressively hot it can be in the desert?

Eventually, though, you cross Raton Pass, which rises more than seven thousand feet above sea level. The air conditioner goes off, the windows come down, green replaces brown, and you get your first glimpse of snow-capped mountains in the distance. You know before long you'll be breathing cooler air during the day and listening to rainfall through the night. Sometimes, I'm tempted to think God must live in the mountains of Colorado. When you hear thunder rolling over the peaks and through the canyons, it's as if He is clearing His throat.

Paul's letter has taken us through some difficult terrain. It started in the dusty flats of spiritual wasteland and has taken us many miles through endless arid prairies. And the desert of Romans 7 was particularly disheartening because it looked so much like the place we were grateful to leave.[7] Fortunately, Paul's letter is a lot like life, particularly for the Christian. Just as hopefulness begins to fade, we enter his Raton Pass.

What the apostle described in his bleak self-portrait is the futility of trying to live the Christian life without the Spirit of God. It's no less futile than trying to earn righteousness apart from faith. We were helpless to overcome the deadly disease of sin without His unmerited favor, and we are equally powerless to please God without His Spirit providing grace. As Paul puts it, "Nothing good dwells in me, that is, in my flesh; for the willing is present in me, but the doing of the good is not" (7:18).

In my own Christian journey, I have discovered that "wretchedness" seems to be a necessary waypoint. Like Paul, I came to a place of utter hopelessness. I felt trapped by my inability to live in a manner that God would find pleasing, a mode of life I genuinely desired. I labored under the weight of condemnation, which is perhaps the most demoralizing feeling a Christian can endure. Nothing will drag you more quickly to a halt and pull you toward sin than shame.

To make matters worse, I was guided by well-meaning people with bad theology. Many churches today preach a gospel that goes strangely silent after one believes in Jesus Christ and only promises to speak again after death. According to this version of the good news, Christians are left to wrestle the flesh on their own until Judgment Day, at which time a tape of their miserable pummeling will be played for all to see just as the pearly gates open to receive them. Strange teaching.

Saved by grace, but sanctified by works? That's not good news.

After reaching my own wretched state, I surrendered to the fact that I am not able to live the Christian life. Only then—having come to the end of myself and not a day sooner—only *then* was I ready to accept the truth of Paul's stunning declaration at the beginning of Romans 8. Like a flash in the darkness, like Raton Pass on the journey to God's dwelling, the truth comes into view: "Therefore there is now no condemnation for those who are in Christ Jesus" (8:1). This is the cardinal truth of every believer's new life "in Christ." This is the truth on which we stand, by which we live, and through which we ultimately achieve victory.

We have reached a significant turning point. From this place forward, the journey will be frequently challenging and sometimes confusing, but never exasperating. From this vantage point, the good news only gets better.

— 8:1–4 —

We must not rush by the first word. The connecting adverb, "therefore," is too important to ignore. It tells us that the statement in verse 1, "There is now no more condemnation for those who are in Christ Jesus," is a continuation of a prior thought.

In the dark desperation of Paul's lonely and futile struggle against the flesh, he cried out, "Who will set me free from the body of this death?" Note the future tense, "*will* set me free." The issue of eternal destiny had already been decided (3:28; 5:1–2; 6:23). The question on Paul's mind was his present struggle. And the answer came: "God through Jesus Christ our Lord [will set me free from the body of this death]." "Therefore, there is *now* no more condemnation ..."

Let me point out three crucial truths derived from 8:1–4:

First, we are eternally secure, *now* as well as when we face judgment (8:1). God has officially declared our justification and He never rescinds His Word.

Second, we are internally free from the control of sin, *now* as well as when we get to heaven (8:2). The Spirit of life has set us free (past tense with ongoing results.)

Third, we are positionally righteous, *now* as well as when we stand before our heavenly Judge (8:3–4). What the Law could not accomplish, God has accomplished on our behalf through His Son.

I appreciate Paul's putting this reassurance up front. It not only consoles the wretched, it frees us to hear and absorb what he has to teach us next. More than once, I've gotten a call from someone about one of our children and I deeply appreciated their saying immediately, "Chuck, let me tell you first that your son/daughter is okay." With my worst fears immediately put to rest, I can hear what needs to be said more clearly.

— 8:5–8 —

When Paul painted his dark self-portrait in chapter 7, we learned about the two natures struggling for control: "the flesh," our old sin nature, and "the Spirit," the gift of God's presence within us. Having been put at ease by the truths in 8:1–4, this struggle looks much different. Even though the old nature never gives up, never backs off, and never concedes defeat, we can live with confident assurance that the Holy Spirit is stronger. Now, the question is, "To whom will we yield control?" Paul's explanation implies a choice on the part of the believer. For simplicity, here is a more literal rendering of the Greek:

> "Those existing according to the flesh set their minds on things of the flesh,
> but,
> those [existing][8] according to Spirit [set their minds on] things of the Spirit."

The next couplet predicts the implications of each choice. Fleshly thinking is death; Spirit thinking is life and peace.

So what is fleshly thinking? What does it mean to "exist according to the flesh?" As always, we allow Scripture to interpret Scripture. Paul's self-portrait describes in painful detail what existing according to the flesh looks like. Existing in the flesh can involve a headlong pursuit of sin. After all, the flesh is hostile to God. Before we received His grace and before His Spirit took up residence within us, the flesh craved only evil. Consequently, Christians have been known to abandon themselves to wrongdoing for a variety of reasons. Some spectators would suggest they were not genuine believers at the time, but we can only speculate. I have been close to one or two people I am reasonably certain were genuine believers but, for a season, behaved like pagans.

In this passage, however, Paul appears to describe something far more common in Christian experience. A believer exists according to the flesh when he or she tries to become righteous by simply trying harder. Remember our study of 3:23 and the illustration of the high jump contest? Those who train hard, expecting to leap into heaven under their own power, will "fall short." That's the old-nature way of thinking. The world system says, "God helps those who help themselves." Grace declares, "A [person] is justified by faith apart from works of the Law" (3:28).

Fleshly thinking can have noble ideals and admirable desires; however, it is also proud to the bone. Fleshly thinking presumes to achieve godly objectives without God. It rejects the grace of God in favor of its own will, its own way, its own ability to do good on its own terms. Fleshly thinking buys into the "self-made man or woman" philosophy and aligns itself remarkably well with the entrepreneurial spirit. While rugged individualism and a "can do" attitude may be good for business, it's death to the spiritual life. It will leave you downright wretched.

However well-intentioned the flesh may appear, we must never forget that it was hostile to God before we received salvation; therefore, we are foolish to think the flesh will cooperate now. The flesh cannot change; it can only be left behind.

—**8:9–11**—

Paul reminds his readers that they are no longer deluded by fleshly thinking, but have gained the capacity to think and choose as a result of their freedom "in Christ." The Spirit of God has given them this freedom. Interestingly, Paul qualifies his assurance, limiting it to those who have received God's grace through faith. Therefore, everything the apostle teaches concerning the believer does not apply to everyone in general. In fact, much of his instruction will appear as nonsense to those who are not "in the Spirit."

Donald Gray Barnhouse has provided a wonderful illustration of the need for the Spirit to give us access to spiritual truths:

> Two men, each accompanied by a dog, meet along a road in the country. The men start to talk and the dogs touch noses and begin to communicate, dog-fashion, with each other. Perhaps they have some way of telling each other that there is a rabbit trail over in the bushes and they romp off together. They come back to their masters and their dog ears hear the sounds of the conversation that is taking place between the two men, but they have not the slightest knowledge of the meaning, whether the men are talking about atomic physics or the price of corn by the bushel. Now what dog knoweth the things of a dog except by the nature of the dog that is within him? Even so the things of a man knoweth no dog, but only the spirit of a man can understand them ... For just as a dog may understand a dog but cannot understand a man, so a man may understand a man but can never understand God, unaided by the Spirit.[9]

—**8:12–13**—

Because the Spirit lives within us and because we have access to the mind of God, we have an obligation. Sounds like work, doesn't it? Some respected, popular theologians teach that the sacrifice of Jesus Christ on our behalf puts us in His debt. They proclaim that while His gift is priceless and we can never repay the cost, we owe Him a debt of gratitude, nonetheless. And this debt demands our complete devotion to do good works until we die ... and perhaps longer.

The Greek word for such teaching is *hogwash*!

We do indeed have an obligation, but it is not to do good things for God. The obligation is to allow the Spirit to do good deeds on our behalf, through us, so that we will become more like Jesus and share the blessings that are due Him. (How great is that?) Paul taught this in Ephesus, Philippi, Colossae, Thessalonica, and perhaps a hundred other places between Jerusalem and Rome. To the Ephesians, he wrote:

> For by grace you have been saved through faith; and that not of yourselves, *it is* the gift of God; not as a result of works, so that no one may boast. For we are His workmanship, created in Christ Jesus for good works, which God prepared beforehand so that we would walk in them. (Eph. 2:8–10)

To the Philippians, he wrote:

> For I am confident of this very thing, that He who began a good work in you will perfect it until the day of Christ Jesus. (Phil. 1:6)

The Lord has good works prepared for us beforehand. He has the desire and the ability to prepare us for those good works. Best of all, He has promised to bring it all together to accomplish what He has determined. Our only responsibility is to let Him. If we do, we live. If we don't, if we give ourselves over to the flesh, then a deathlike, miserable existence is our inevitable end.

—8:14–17—

Paul has focused on the negative (telling what *not* to do) long enough. He quickly turns to the positive. In each of the next four verses, we find a practical benefit of living in the Spirit.

The first benefit: practical everyday leading from God (8:14). This is frequently used as a proof text to support the notion that believers receive either verbal or nonverbal messages from the Holy Spirit telling them what decisions to make or what to do next. This is *not* Paul's teaching here. This actually shortchanges the promises of the new covenant. As we will learn by the end of this chapter, the Lord will do something far more profound, far more useful than merely whispering commands in our spirit's ear. In fact, Paul's next statement assures us that the Holy Spirit is a gift, not a dictator.

Note how Paul phrases the sentence: "For all who are being led by the Spirit of God, these are sons of God." Many turn it around to support their predetermined conclusion: "The sons of God are led by the Spirit." But this would not be a true statement. While the Lord is certainly faithful to lead genuine believers, most are either too distracted or too stubborn to follow, so they aren't really going anywhere. Paul's teaching in other portions of Scripture makes it clear that the Spirit does lead, but the believer may elect to go his or her own way, thus "grieving" Him (Eph. 4:30).

This verse is both a promise and a practical means of assurance. Those who are actively following the Spirit will bear the unmistakable evidence of that leading (see Gal. 5:18–25). When that evidence—or "fruit," as Paul likes to call it—is visible, it assures the believer that he or she is indeed a "son of God."

By the way, we shouldn't replace the word "son" with "child," even for women.

Paul could have chosen the neutral Greek term for child, but he deliberately chose "son" to indicate that believers stand to inherit something. Women are "sons of God" because they, no less than men, are a part of God's estate.

The second benefit: fearless intimacy with God (8:15). Paul again reinforces the good news that believers have been emancipated. They no longer serve a master who tells them what to do, when to do it, how long, how often, and where. We have been freed and therefore we are free indeed. God has purchased us. The payment was His Son's death. While He had every right to own us as slaves, He tore the bill of sale into shreds and drafted a new document: adoption papers! He is not merely a kinder, gentler Master; He is our "Abba." That's the Aramaic term of endearment for one's father. It's the closest word we have to the name "Daddy."

Intimacy with the Almighty Creator of the universe! What an awesome thought.

We have an obligation, not as slaves repaying a debt, but as sons, who have a genuine stake in our Daddy's estate. The obligation doesn't come as orders from the Big House, whispered secretly from Spirit to spirit, but as an invitation to become a contributing member of a family. If we do good, it is not for His sake alone, but for ours and for everyone else's in God's household.

The third benefit: assurance of belonging to God (8:16). If the Holy Spirit speaks into the souls of His beloved sons, it's only to say this: "You are my precious child."

This is the only place the New Testament we are told that the Holy Spirit speaks in a prophetic way *as a general practice.* After Jesus inaugurated the new covenant (which we will examine later), the Lord spoke through designated people. He spoke prophetically through apostles and prophets until the last of the New Testament books, the book of Revelation, was written by the last remaining apostle, John.

Some critics object to this, pointing to the fact that the Bible is replete with stories of God speaking to, and through, people, and that He still has the power to do so. This is true. The Lord specifically chose some to be His spokespeople for a given time and for a defined purpose. But, as one insightful commentator states, what is *narrative* is not necessarily *normative.* Just because someone in the Bible has experienced something doesn't mean we should expect it will become a common occurrence.

Balaam's donkey, for instance, under the supernatural direction of God, rebuked his master (Num. 22:28–30). The event took place in the Bible, the Lord still has the ability to speak through anything He chooses, and there's nothing to prevent Him from doing it again. Nevertheless, I recommend we keep to our Bibles instead of visiting barnyards to hear the voice of God.

We need no other prophetic utterance until the end-time events begin to unfold. We have all the information we need. Truth be told, we have more than we can handle in a lifetime as it is! This is not to say that we're on our own or that the

Spirit does not lead. He is with us and He leads us. (We will soon learn from the apostle how the Spirit leads.) However, at this stage in the timeline of redemption, God does not speak prophetically to, or through, people. That is one of the major tenants of the Reformation (*sola scriptura*) and something that, in part, defines us as Protestant. We have no need of popes, neither in Rome nor next door, nor do we need night visions. We have God's Word in black print on white paper, accessible in multiple languages, and understandable to all. I suggest we keep our focus there.

The fourth benefit: a continual reminder of our value before God (8:17). Adoption was a common practice in Roman law. Much of Roman society depended on a system called "patronage," in which one person became a "godfather" to less powerful people. This person, in turn, owed allegiance to his patron. Frequently, a patron would adopt a favorite unrelated client to inherit his estate. When Paul spoke of "adoption as sons," his Roman readers would have immediately recalled that Caesar Augustus received much of his power through adoption by his patron, Julius Caesar, the founding father of the Roman Empire.

Through adoption, believers have become coheirs with God's one and only Son. And through our identification with Him, we stand to inherit everything that is due Him. Fast forward to Revelation 5:12 to see what that entails. He will share everything with His adopted brothers and sisters … all, that is, except worship. That is His alone.

Paul took great pains to convince believers that only unbelieving people exist according to the flesh and that only sons and daughters of God exist according to the Spirit. A natural reaction to that truth is to say, "Then I want to live by the Spirit! How do I do that?" And I will admit that my first inclination was to comb that passage for applications. But I found no imperatives; no commands, no "should" or "should nots," not even a helpful suggestion. The apostle didn't describe what kind of behavior will help us "exist according to the Spirit" or prescribe a seven-step plan to becoming more spiritual.

To be honest, I found that frustrating. I confess that, in my flesh, I tried to turn this Spirit-led life into a self-made holiness. Suddenly, I found myself back in chapter 7 and I began to feel that telltale, wretched ache all over again. Then I was reminded that the flesh is ever with us and, oh, how it wants to be in control!

Instead of citing a list of deeds that result in holiness, Paul assures us that the Spirit of God decides on His own to start living in and through believers. Then he describes what the Spirit will do for us and the blessings we will receive as a result! Existing in the Spirit is not about what we do for Him; remember … we can do nothing. The Spirit life is about what He will do on our behalf, because the indwelling presence of God's Spirit is a gift of grace. The same gift that redeems us from slavery to sin also rescues us from it. The free gift of salvation from sin begins now, not after we've gone to the grave.

So, what must we do? What is our obligation? The answer is uncomplicated. Difficult to do because the flesh will not surrender control easily, but the answer is straightforward enough: *Nothing*.

Nothing?! You don't have to pray? You don't have to get up at 4 a.m. for a "quiet time"? You don't have to have family devotions? You don't have to give away all your money, or shower every day, or obey the Ten Commandments, or wear dark clothing, or eat low-fat foods, or do a pile of good deeds to become more spiritual?

No. Nothing. If you have the Spirit within you, you are as spiritual as you're ever going to be.

If there is an imperative to be found in Paul's description of the Spirit life, it is to quit *trying so hard* to be spiritual. Stop all of that. Instead, let the Spirit be spiritual. When that makes sense to you, you can be sure you're setting your mind on the things of the Spirit ... and you're starting to understand grace. Until then, you will not be ready to accept Paul's teaching in the latter half of his letter to the Romans.

Glorying and Groaning (Romans 8:18–27)

¹⁸For I consider that the sufferings of this present time are not worthy to be compared with the glory that is to be revealed to us. ¹⁹For the anxious longing of the creation waits eagerly for the revealing of the sons of God. ²⁰For the creation was subjected to futility, not willingly, but because of Him who subjected it, in hope ²¹that the creation itself also will be set free from its slavery to corruption into the freedom of the glory of the children of God. ²²For we know that the whole creation groans and suffers the pains of childbirth together until now. ²³And not only this, but also we ourselves, having the first fruits of the Spirit, even we ourselves groan within ourselves, waiting eagerly for *our* adoption as sons, the redemption of our body. ²⁴For in hope we have been saved, but hope that is seen is not hope; for who hopes for what he *already* sees? ²⁵But if we hope for what we do not see, with perseverance we wait eagerly for it.
²⁶In the same way the Spirit also helps our weakness; for we do not know how to pray as we should, but the Spirit Himself intercedes for *us* with groanings too deep for words; ²⁷and He who searches the hearts knows what the mind of the Spirit is, because He intercedes for the saints according to *the will of* God.

In 1957, I was eight thousand miles away from home in Southeast Asia, bunked up with forty-seven other Marines in a Quonset hut, and lonely for my wife. We had been married only two and a half years—practically newlyweds—so, Okinawa was *not* where I wanted to be, and I very much resented God for putting me there. Fortunately, another man had chosen to be there and served his Master through an organization called The Navigators. One particularly lonely evening, he placed a gift in my hands that would change everything for me … starting with me.

I sat on my bunk and slid an attractively bound volume out of its protective covering to read the front: *The Amplified New Testament.* Until that time, the only versions available were the old King James and the J. B. Phillips translation, but this was brand new and unique. I broke it open that Christmas night and sat perusing familiar passages in the solitude of the empty barracks, for how long, I don't know. When I came across Philippians 3:10, the amplified verse impacted me so profoundly, I decided it would be my focus for the new year.

As Paul shared his enthusiasm for ministry and the gospel with his brothers and sisters in Philippi, his passion reached a climax with a statement of his purpose in life:

> [For my determined purpose is] that I may know Him [that I may progressively become more deeply and intimately acquainted with Him, perceiving and recognizing and understanding the wonders of His Person more strongly and more clearly], and that I may in that same way come to know the power outflowing from His resurrection [which it exerts over believers], and that I may so share His sufferings as to be continually transformed [in spirit into His likeness even] to His death. (Phil. 3:10 Amplified)

In January, I focused on the first few phrases. "[For my determined purpose is] that I may know Him [that I may progressively become more deeply and intimately acquainted with Him]." For the entire month of January, I would focus my time and attention on knowing Him deeply, intimately, and progressively. I spent extended time with Him, I talked with Him through the day by prayer, and I tried to think like I imagined He would. I would turn in at night, mentally focused on Him.

In February, I concentrated on the next portion: " … that I may in that same way come to know the power outflowing from His resurrection [which it exerts over believers]." I thought, *Lord, if You could give me that kind of dynamic. Who knows? I might be able to speak to one of my buddies here about Jesus. So I give you this part of the verse for my February of 1958.* Before the year ended, seven came to know Christ. While that might not seem significant, a lot of people would consider seven out of forty-eight in a Marine Corps Quonset hut a revival! So, the eight of us formed a small Bible study group and committed ourselves to a Scripture memory program. We attended a GI fellowship on Friday nights and worked our way through the little InterVarsity hymnal. I committed to memory a lot of those great hymns. It was one incredible year.

In March, I concentrated on the phrase "that I may so share His sufferings." I don't mind telling you that the phrase didn't go down well. The resentment I felt toward the Lord for landing me on an island had diminished some, mostly because of my missionary friend, but it had not been completely resolved.

Many people come to Christ in the hope that all their troubles will evaporate once they believe and begin following Him. A lot of popular preachers proclaim that false gospel, a doctrine they call the "Word of Faith." I had been a Christian for many years by that time, but I still expected the Lord to make things easy for those He redeems and calls "sons." Placing the entire globe between a newlywed couple felt cruel to me, and I struggled to find His goodness in my circumstances.

Few people have enjoyed a more intimate relationship with God than Paul. Few have experienced the joy that he reported in his letters throughout his ministry. Yet few have suffered more than he. His unguarded words to the believers in Corinth summarize just some of his hardships.

> Are they servants of Christ?—I speak as if insane—I more so; in far more labors, in far more imprisonments, beaten times without number, often in danger of death. Five times I received from the Jews thirty-nine *lashes*. Three times I was beaten with rods, once I was stoned, three times I was shipwrecked, a night and a day I have spent in the deep. *I have been* on frequent journeys, in dangers from rivers, dangers from robbers, dangers from *my* countrymen, dangers from the Gentiles, dangers in the city, dangers in the wilderness, dangers on the sea, dangers among false brethren; *I have been* in labor and hardship, through many sleepless nights, in hunger and thirst, often without food, in cold and exposure. Apart from *such* external things, there is the daily pressure on me *of* concern for all the churches. (2 Cor. 11:23–28)

Experience is sometimes the most convincing authority a teacher can have. Paul's body bore the scars of suffering for the sake of Christ and each mark commemorated a victory to Him. Perhaps no other person on earth could have encouraged the Romans so effectively. Having assured his readers that the Lord will be faithful to complete in them what He started, Paul needs to address an obvious question. "If there is now no more condemnation, and if I am now a son of God, why do I feel as if I'm being punished?"

—8:18—

Paul has just declared that the Holy Spirit continually affirms the believer's place in God's family as one of His children (8:16). Furthermore, we stand to share

Christ's inheritance, which includes both blessing and suffering, glorying and groaning (8:17). While the apostle does not minimize the intensity of our present distress—including his own, which was more severe than most—he considers it a mere fraction of the future splendor we will enjoy forever.

Alan Redpath wrote in his book *The Making of a Man of God*, "There is no victory without a fight, and there is no battle without wounds."[10] I'm not suggesting that we must pay for our glory with groaning or that sanctification can be purchased with suffering. Throughout Christian history, well-meaning men and women have literally beaten themselves with rods and whips in the hope of overcoming the flesh and gaining for themselves more Spirit. Some of these "flagellants" discovered later that sanctification didn't hurt as much if they wore a thick leather jacket under their clothing, which is, of course, absurd. Neither senseless pain nor going through the motions of self-deprecation puts someone on the fast track to spiritual maturity.

We don't need to go looking for suffering. Just living authentically in the Spirit under the tyranny of a fallen world, as He did, will bring enough suffering on its own. And that affliction allows us to share some measure of His experience. After all, He warned us that the world would afflict us as it did Him, for no other reason than our breaking ranks with evil (John 15:18–20). So, in a practical sense, suffering tells us we're on the right path. As F. B. Meyer stated in his book *Christ in Isaiah*, "If in an unknown country, I am informed that I must pass a valley where the sun is hidden, or over a stony bit of road, to reach my abiding-place—when I come to it, each moment of shadow or jolt of the carriage tells me I am on the right road."[11]

"Although He was a Son, [Jesus] learned obedience from the things which He suffered" (Heb. 5:8), and obedience led Him to die a torturous death. Paul followed Christ down the path of suffering and it led to martyrdom. In this section of his letter, the apostle bids us to follow him as he follows Christ.

— **8:19–22** —

Our suffering after adoption as sons is not the result of senseless beating by God either. While the Creator remains sovereign over His creation, the bad things that happen to us are *not* His original desire. He did not create these bodies to endure pain, or to wither under disease, or to crave evil. God created us to worship and enjoy Him forever; therefore, death is the ultimate affront to His creative act. Death is the result of sin, a perversion of His original design ... an enemy (see 1 Cor. 15:26).

The story of Creation concludes with a pristine world in which every blade of grass is jade green, every stream is crystal clear, every tree laden with fruit. God pronounces it all "good" and then gives it to His first children, Adam and Eve, as an inheritance to steward (Gen. 1:27–30). But then the children of God exchange the truth for a lie, they sell their inheritance as sons for bondage as slaves, and they open the door for disease, disaster, death, and decay to enter God's once-idyllic world. Paul personifies here creation as moaning in desperate, anguished anticipation of a future event: "the revealing of the sons of God" (8:19).

Note how he chooses to describe this future event. Not, "the revealing of God's plan," which, of course, it will be. Not even "the revealing of God's Son," as will certainly occur. But the revealing of the *sons of God*, which bears the subtle suggestion that the identity of the sons remains a mystery. We will undoubtedly be surprised to discover some among the saints we thought to be pagan, and others, who were admired as spiritual giants, missing! Furthermore, it's no coincidence that Paul chooses the Greek word *apokalypsis*—from which we derive our word "apocalypse"—to describe this event. It is the time when Jesus returns to set all things right again.

When humankind fell, creation fell. When God restores the believing remnant of humanity, creation will be restored. The Lord Himself will rule as King, the desert will blossom like a rose, the lamb and the lion will lie down together, and sin will have no place. Until then, we live in the meantime. Until that day, creation groans in anguished expectation like a mother in labor. Verses 19–22 reveals four important facts about the groaning of creation:

> The groaning of creation is temporary. (8:19)
> The groaning of creation is a consequence of sin. (8:20)
> The groaning of creation is a means to an end. (8:20–21)
> The groaning of creation is universal. (8:22)

—8:23–25—

Because we are an integral part of creation, we too groan. We groan through the inescapable hardships of life in fallen creation: tragedies of financial ruin, broken relationships, nature's disasters, terminal illness, and inevitable death. Moreover, we groan as the drag of the flesh keeps us from enjoying complete and uninterrupted intimacy with our Creator. We are like children in an orphanage, waiting with bags packed and completed adoption papers in hand for the coming of our Father … whom we can call "Daddy" (8:15).

Paul again used the Greek term *elpis* ("hope") to describe the "assured expectation" (5:2–5) of our inevitable future. While we have been adopted and redeemed, there is an aspect of those gifts that remains to be fulfilled. In this "assured expectation" we have been saved, but we are citizens of another King though living in hostile territory, living behind enemy lines, as it were. We have only received the "first fruits" of our salvation.

People who derive their living from the land understand the concept of "first fruits." They toil against weeds, drought, pests, and the weather's extremes to grow a crop. They drop their seeds into the ground or tend their trees and vines with no guarantees. So, the first sign of yield is cause for celebration. Furthermore, the quality of that first fruit is an indication of how the rest of the season will go. If the first ear of corn, bushel of apples, bunch of grapes, or bundle of wheat is of excellent quality, the people who labored over it breathe a sigh of relief. All they need to do is protect the crop and wait for it to ripen. They persevere and eagerly wait for it (cf. 8:23).

In addition to groaning through the turmoil of life and its inevitable heartaches, we also groan because of the flesh and its continual drag on the life we long to enjoy. Our bodies and our natural way of thinking are a part of creation, which is no less twisted now as when Adam and Eve brought death and decay into the world through sin. So, we groan inwardly as the civil war between the old nature and new nature drags on.

—8:26-27—

"In the same way . . ." In the same way as what? The answer is found in the progression of Paul's teaching from 8:19 to this point. Creation groans (8:19–22) and we groan within ourselves (8:23–25); in the same way, the Spirit also groans (8:26). He groans on our behalf because, like the Son, the Spirit has taken the problem of evil upon Himself, voluntarily, by dwelling within His children. Jesus promised His followers that another being would come to be with them in their struggles—a comforter, a teacher, an advocate. He promised His Holy Spirit. Not only does the Spirit convict us of sin and teach truth, He endures our suffering with us. He has been "called alongside" (a literal translation of the Greek term *paraklētos*, or Paraclete in English) to help us endure.

When I am tempted to think that God is cruel to leave us in our suffering, I remember that He, too, moans with "groanings too deep for words." When I see a mother sobbing over the dead body of her child, I know the Holy Spirit suffers her anguish too. When I see a man kiss the cold cheek of his bride and give her body to the care of a mortician, I know the Holy Spirit feels his desperate ache. He is the Spirit of the Creator, who made these bodies to reflect His glory, not suffer

From My Journal

Praying without Words

I can remember one particular struggle that kept me on my knees for weeks. My prayers started out with my outlining a reasonable plan of action for the Lord to follow. But as the difficulty continued, I realized He could see issues that were hidden to me and He could account for infinite variables that I could not (Isa. 55:8–9). So, I decided it was best to leave the "how" in His hands and concentrate on requesting my desired outcome. As the difficulty dragged on, I began to accept that my desired outcome might not be the right resolution, so I surrendered that to the Lord as well. This particular burden eventually brought me to the end of my own strength and left me in a listless heap, too exhausted for prayer. My suffering overwhelmed my capacity for speech, so all I could express to God as the turmoil intensified were pleading moans—emotions too intense for words.

I admit that I often don't understand the Lord. I cannot fathom why He would allow me to suffer so much for so long when, in an instant, with a mere word, He could resolve the issue and end my sorrow. He seemed distant and uncaring at that particular time, so I made it a discipline to remind myself of His wisdom and goodness.

> The ways of the LORD are right,
> And the righteous will walk in them,
> But transgressors will stumble in them. (Hos. 14:9)

At the end of all reason, after my strength had been drained and my words fell silent, when anguished emotions seeped through every pore of my body and left me dry, I lay submitted to His will and His way. And I rested in the assurance that while I had no words and did not know what to pray, the Spirit of God had been interceding on my behalf. He was doing what I could not.

When my difficulty ended, the Lord resolved many issues far more effectively than I could have imagined. He left some matters unresolved, of course, but I trust His judgment. More importantly, I was changed, and undoubtedly for the better. I emerged from my trial serenely submitted to God's will, a posture I find much easier after my ordeal. For that, I am grateful.

I have the distinct feeling I am not alone in the struggle I have just described.

disease, disaster, death, and decay. He loves us even more than we love ourselves, and therefore He groans with us.

Fortunately, the Holy Spirit possesses power we do not. At the end of our strength, we groan and that's it. There's nothing more. The Spirit groans with a purpose. He intercedes on our behalf, praying with wisdom we do not possess, requesting for us what we are too shortsighted to perceive. And — most important of all — He groans His intercessions in heaven so that our minds and the mind of the Father will unite to accomplish His will.

Sixteen months in Okinawa was not my will. Stationed in San Francisco, I had a beautiful young bride, a wonderful little apartment, an enviable post with the Marine Corps, and a delightful opportunity to cultivate our marriage. I had it made! Then came the telegram that ruined all of that. Sitting on my bunk all alone that Christmas night in a cold Quonset hut, I felt abandoned by the Lord. That is, until He confronted me with a life-changing question I would never have heard in the commotion of my happiness back in the States: "Do you want to know Me?"

Because of Paul's letter, I know the Holy Spirit groaned through my loneliness and disappointment with me. But where I would have given up all hope of joy, He interceded for me, praying the Father's will into my life on my behalf. The Spirit tugged me in the direction of God's plan for my future, a ministry I could never have imagined and would have certainly missed if I had selfishly pursued my own agenda. A. W. Tozer wrote, "It is doubtful whether God can bless a man greatly until He has hurt him deeply."[12] I wish there was an easier, more pleasant way to prepare a heart to receive joy — some means other than crushing. If there were, our God of love would certainly use it.

Looking back, sixteen months was a short time compared to the hardship of others. Those sixteen months of groaning prepared me to receive more than forty-five years of joy in ministry. The return has far exceeded the suffering. Today I can barely imagine what my short seventy-plus years on earth will yield in eternity!

Application

Groaning . . . then Glory!

The problem of evil is difficult for everyone. Unbelievers struggle to comprehend how a good, all-powerful God can allow evil to continue. Believers begin to question everything when the intensity of sorrow or suffering becomes unbearable. Even creation itself groans in anguished anticipation for disease, disaster, death, and decay to end. Nevertheless, Paul considers this present suffering to be minor when compared to the glory of eternity (8:17–25).

As I have taught and lived this portion of Scripture for the better part of half a century, I observe two principles at work.

First, *the greater the groan, the greater the glory*. God is not the source of pain and He did not promise to prevent our suffering. Instead, He promises that no pain will go to waste. What the world intends for harm, God will use for our good. Not only will He make us more like His Son, He will use afflictions to give us a greater capacity for future blessing.

When you find yourself afflicted and suffering, rest assured that however deeply you hurt, your joy will be greater when the trial ends. Therefore, endure with hope—confident assurance.

Second, *the weaker our spirit, the stronger His support*. I recall many times when I barely had the strength to stand in the pulpit on Sunday. One Friday afternoon, our daughter fell to the pavement from a cheerleading pyramid and broke her back. For the next thirty-six hours—Friday night, Saturday, and Saturday night—we sat by her hospital bed praying that her paralysis wouldn't be permanent. With her long-term condition still uncertain, I preached as scheduled on Sunday. I blinked through tears and somehow made my way through the sermon, which surely flopped. Or so I thought. The recording of that particular sermon ultimately became the most requested of any I had delivered in that church. Why? I am convinced that it was because I preached it in utter weakness.

When affliction and suffering bring you to your knees, that is when the power of God has the greatest effect in your ministry (2 Cor. 12:10). I don't mean to suggest that taking a step back from work isn't sometimes necessary. You should be fit to serve. However, when you do continue ministering to others in the midst of suffering, God multiplies His power in your weakness.

Let me boil this down to several practical dos and don'ts:

Don't assume your suffering is the result of God's punishment.
Do expect that when the suffering ends, He will give you even greater joy.
Don't assume the Lord has abandoned you.
Do confess your fear and doubt and ask Him for strength to press on.
Don't assume you have been rejected or forsaken by God.
Do remain faithful to your duties, even if you must reduce your load for
    the time being.
Don't assume your prayers are not heard.
Do continue praying, even when you don't know what to say.

Don't assume that your suffering gives you permission to give up.

Do trust that the Lord will magnify His strength through your weakness.

Jesus warned His followers that the world will hate them on His account and mistreatment will mark their days as certainly as it did His. Nevertheless, His experience established the pattern for us. "In the days of His flesh, [Jesus] offered up both prayers and supplications with loud crying and tears to the One able to save Him from death, and He was heard because of His piety. Although He was a Son, He learned obedience from the things which He suffered" (Heb. 5:7–8). He shared in our suffering; soon we shall share in His glory! How great is *that*!

We Overwhelmingly Conquer (Romans 8:28–39)

28And we know that God causes all things to work together for good to those who love God, to those who are called according to *His* purpose. 29For those whom He foreknew, He also predestined *to become* conformed to the image of His Son, so that He would be the firstborn among many brethren; 30and these whom He predestined, He also called; and these whom He called, He also justified; and these whom He justified, He also glorified.

31What then shall we say to these things? If God *is* for us, who *is* against us? 32He who did not spare His own Son, but delivered Him over for us all, how will He not also with Him freely give us all things? 33Who will bring a charge against God's elect? God is the one who justifies; 34who is the one who condemns? Christ Jesus is He who died, yes, rather who was raised, who is at the right hand of God, who also intercedes for us. 35Who will separate us from the love of Christ? Will tribulation, or distress, or persecution, or famine, or nakedness, or peril, or sword? 36Just as it is written,

> "For Your sake we are being put to death all day long;
> We were considered as sheep to be slaughtered."

37But in all these things we overwhelmingly conquer through Him who loved us. 38For I am convinced that neither death, nor life, nor angels, nor principalities, nor things present, nor things to come, nor powers, 39nor height, nor depth, nor any other created thing, will be able to separate us from the love of God, which is in Christ Jesus our Lord.

Many years ago, Rod Serling penned an episode of *The Twilight Zone* in which a kindly antique dealer happened to release a genie from an otherwise worthless bottle. In keeping with tradition, the man was granted wishes — a generous four wishes—but warned by the genie to choose wisely. After wasting one wish on something insignificant and then consulting his wife, the man called for money, one million dollars to be exact, which the genie granted immediately. After giving away nearly $60,000 to their needy friends, the man and his wife eagerly totaled the balance of their nest egg. Unfortunately, before they could finish, the IRS auditor handed them a bill for all but five dollars of what remained.

He should have wished for one million tax-free dollars. He failed to consider the consequences of his wish and to wish accordingly.

Next, he wished for power, to be the leader of a modern, powerful country in which he could not be voted out of office. The genie immediately granted his request and, in a flash, he found himself in a bunker, surrounded by Nazi attendants and sporting a style of mustache that will never come back.

He should have considered the genie's fondness for irony and been more specific.

The poor man had no alternative but to use his final wish to restore life as it was. The temporarily rich and powerful shopkeeper gained only wisdom from the experience. He learned, firsthand, that the power to wish without complete foreknowledge could be the making of his own hell. If only he had found a genie who genuinely cared about him.

In describing the problem of evil that continues to afflict the world as a result of sin, Paul has highlighted two human limitations that tend to make matters worse. First, "we do not see" (8:25). Our perspective is limited. We see nothing of the future and can never predict what will occur only a few minutes ahead. Second, "we do not know how to pray as we should" (8:26). We may do our very best to pray in harmony with God's will, but we frequently wish for the very opposite of what is good for us. Fortunately, we do not have an evil genie for a god. And I cannot count the number of times I have thanked my Lord for *not* granting an earlier, short-sighted request!

— **8:28** —

We do not see and we do not know how to pray as we ought; however, we do know one all-important fact. The verse doesn't begin, "We hope," "We suppose," or "We wish," but rather "We know." We have a promise founded upon the character of our Creator: "To those who love God, He works together all things into good, to the ones who are called according to His purpose" (my literal translation). Paul cautiously chooses his words and arranges them carefully to state this foundational promise. Each phrase warrants closer examination.

To those who love God. The Greek language places great importance on word order. Paul places this phrase at the beginning of the clause to stress that the promise is intended for believers. While the Lord acts in the best interest of everyone, He makes this particular promise exclusively to His very own "sons."

He works together. The term Paul uses is a compound of "with" and "work." It conveys the idea of a weaver carefully interlacing strands of colored cloth into a preplanned pattern.

All things. Greek writers frequently used this term to refer to the universe, all things both seen and unseen, good and bad, real and even imagined. God utilizes everything—including the evil deeds of evil people.

Into good. The preposition "into" carries the idea of space, as though all things are being corralled by His sovereign will. A good rendering might use "unto," which reflects His accomplishing a specific purpose, but I prefer "into." He not only has a purpose in mind as He weaves all things, He will achieve a result. And it will be good.

Our flesh would have us believe that the "good" God causes *our* good, that is, what will give us happiness, contentment, or joy. But this is only partially true. Throughout Romans, Paul uses the term "good" almost exclusively in a moral sense. "Good" is that which pleases God because it reflects His nature and conforms to His original created order. In the beginning, He created the world good, and at the end of days, the world will be recreated good.

God's "good" is not completely focused on humanity; however, people are happy, content, and joyful when they live in His goodness and with Him in proper perspective.

To the ones who are called according to His purpose. These people are identical to "those who love God." Jesus said, "If you love Me, you will keep My commandments" (John 14:15), and "So that the world may know that I love the Father, I do exactly as the Father commanded Me" (14:31). Love for God and following His commands are inexorably linked.

Putting it all back together, we have: "For those who love God, the Lord sovereignly weaves the strands of every circumstance, every influence, every atom or idea they encounter for the purpose of creating moral good within them—those whom He has called to join His redemptive plan for the world."

When the Lord restores His universe, it will be even better than His original design. And His restoration begins with His people. To accomplish His plan in each of us, He orchestrates all things, including disease, disaster, death, and decay. The world's destructive designs then become tools in the hand of the Almighty, who will turn them to accomplish His good.

Does this mean that all things in the world are good? Clearly, they are not. The world is unfair, brutal, shocking, and demoralizing, and it includes people who relentlessly oppose God's created order. Nevertheless, as evil tries to destroy, the Lord turns the world's destruction into our gain.

If God uses evil for His purposes, does this mean He brings evil on His people? Never! God is not the author of sin. Only good things come from God. He does not bring evil into the world; we do that through sin and, as a race, we perpetuate suffering through continued sin. The Lord merely allows humanity and the world to continue living as they choose, but never beyond His sovereign control over creation.

— 8:29–30 —

Nothing will subvert or alter the plans of God. The destiny of each believer is what Paul earlier called "good," which he further defined as "conformed to the image of His Son." This gives the apostle an opportunity to reveal another confidence-building truth. Having shown the Christians in Rome the destination of their spiritual path, he turns them to look in the direction from which they came.

Foreknew ▸ Predestined to be like Christ ▸ Called ▸ Justified ▸ 👤 ▸ Glorified

God foreknew them, which is to say, He knew them intimately through active involvement in their lives. The Greek verb *ginōskō* (which is the equivalent of the Hebrew verb, *yada*) describes a scrutinizing knowledge that goes beyond mere awareness. The verb was a common euphemism for sexual intimacy shared between a married couple.

Those whom God foreknew in this active sense do not include everyone. This has led some to suggest that God deliberately passed over some, electing them to damnation. That may be a logical inference, but we must be careful not to take Scripture beyond what it actually says. This is Paul's teaching about believers; he isn't commenting on nonbelievers at this point.

Those God foreknew, *He predestined*. This Greek term is based on the same word we studied in 1:1, in which Paul wrote that he had been "set apart" (*aphorizō*), or as I had playfully suggested, "off-horizoned." The root word *horizō* means "to limit, appoint, determine." The prefix *pro*, of course, indicates that the action was done ahead of time, as when someone is "*pro*active." Those the Lord knew intimately and actively, He appointed in advance to become like Jesus in their character. Thus, the one and only Son of God will become, as it were, the eldest brother of all those the Father has adopted.

Those God predestined are *called to believe*, and those who believe *are justified* (3:21–5:21). Eventually, all believers *will be glorified*, which does not involve exaltation like a hero; it is to be like Christ. To be glorified is to have both pure character and a body that cannot be harmed by the world any longer.

—8:31–36—

Paul continues his encouragement by asking the rhetorical question, "What shall we say to these things?" I understand "these things" to be the summation of Paul's teaching to this point: the depravity of humankind (1:19–3:20), justification by grace through faith (3:21–5:21), and sanctification by the Holy Spirit (6:1–8:30). As the believer considers the course of salvation, he cannot miss the proactive role of God in bringing him or her along the path.

Foreknew ▸ Predestined to be like Christ ▸ Called ▸ Justified ▸ Glorified

Paul's use of the provisional term "if" assumes the condition to be true for the sake of argument. Therefore, the term "because" can be inserted to render the verse: "Because God is for us, who can be against us?"

He asks, in effect, "Because God proactively foreknew and predestined believers to be like His Son, and then faithfully called and justified us, will He not be faithful to complete the final step?" This leads Paul to reassure his readers by asking and answering four rhetorical questions, much like an orator stirring a crowd into a frenzy. Each question takes clear aim at Satan and his minions, but demands the same response: "No one!" for evil is powerless before Almighty God.

Who is against us? (8:31)
Who will bring a charge against God's elect? (8:33)
Who is the one who condemns? (8:34)
Who will separate us from the love of Christ? (8:35)

Who shall oppose us? (8:31). Make no mistake about it; there is plenty to oppose us in life. Hardships and tragedies relentlessly batter away at the hope of all believers. Persecutors and naysayers oppose us. Indwelling sin opposes us. Fear of loss opposes us. The evil one and those who serve him oppose us. And, eventually, death opposes us. But what are they compared to the power of God?

If anyone doubts the Lord's faithfulness, Paul cites the fact that He has already sacrificed His Son to redeem us, to emancipate us from slavery. With the price paid, it makes no sense for Him to refuse to take delivery on what He has purchased. And having completely committed His greatest object of love, why would

He then hold back what He values far less than His Son? Let me illustrate the absurdity this way:

Let's say the manager of a local jewelry store called one afternoon to let you know your name had been entered in a drawing and that you are the winner of a very expensive diamond necklace. "All you need to do is come to the store at ten o'clock tomorrow and receive your prize!"

So, you arrive the following morning shortly before ten to find a small crowd gathered around a presentation platform. After a few comments, the manager places the necklace around your neck for a few photographs, everyone applauds, and the ceremony ends. You have your gift, but you don't want to wear it home, so you kindly ask the manager, "May I have a box for this beautiful necklace? I want to keep it safe for the trip home."

No manager on earth would respond, "No! We gave you the necklace, the box is your responsibility!" The cost of a box is nothing compared to the necklace.

We have everything we need in Christ, and the Father will withhold nothing to protect His children and to bring them safely to Himself.

Who will bring a charge against God's elect? (8:33). This is a legal question. The Greek term translated "bring a charge against" means simply "to call in." It's an official summons to appear in court to face an accusation.

I remember standing in the front row of the church I was pastoring years ago, singing along with the congregation shortly before I was to preach. A grim-looking man in a suit entered the back of the sanctuary and slowly walked toward the front. I thought he would slip into one of the rows, take a hymnal, and join the singing, but he kept walking. He came all the way to the front, faced me, and slapped an envelope against my chest. It was a summons!

I read it over and quickly determined it was another nut with a frivolous case, but it still unnerved me. Something about being called before a judge puts a knot in my stomach, even if I know I'm legally faultless. I have this nagging worry that a particularly slick lawyer might be able to fool the court.

Now suppose the only judge with any jurisdiction happened to be my father. The nut's frivolous charge would stand no chance of even getting a hearing.

Any charge brought against us will not stand up in court. Because our debt for sin has been paid in full, we are unimpeachable. We are and forever will be considered just before the Judge of heaven.

Who is the one who condemns? (8:34). When I received the summons, I knew the charge was frivolous. I trusted that a judge would take one look and throw the case out, and that would be the end of it. (That's exactly what happened.) A false accusation is difficult to bear, but at least I had justice on my side. I can face an unjust accuser without fear as long as a just judge will hear the case. But what if the judge is against you? What hope do you have?

Paul's answer highlights four great Christian doctrines:

"Christ Jesus is He who died." That's the doctrine of *substitution*. The Son of God paid the debt of sin on our behalf.

"Who was raised . . ." That's the doctrine of *resurrection*. The Son of God was raised to new life and, by our identification with Him, we too have new life.

"Who is at the right hand of God . . ." That's the doctrine of *accession*. The Son of God has received title to the entire universe and now rules as its king and ultimate judge.

"Who also intercedes for us." That's the doctrine of *intercession*. The Son of God is our advocate, our representative in heaven, faithfully looking out for our welfare.

So, we have the Father, who sacrificed His one and only Son to free us from bondage to sin. We have the Son, who paid the price to set us free and now holds title to everything. And we have the Holy Spirit, who lives within us to share our suffering and to be the spiritual driving force we cannot. With the triune God working for us on all sides, what possible chance does any form of evil stand?

Who will separate us from the love of Christ? (8:35–36). Paul suggests no less than seven possibilities, all of which he has personally endured (2 Cor. 11:23–28). And let's be honest. When we suffer the afflictions of pressure, prejudice, persecution, or poverty, we naturally begin to wonder if the Lord still cares about us or even remembers we're alive. Our flesh feels nurtured when it's most comfortable, and it feels abandoned during hardship. To reassure his readers of God's love, Paul quotes Psalm 44:22 to remind his readers that hardship has always been the experience of God's faithful followers.

After having a medical procedure, I always appreciate the physician telling me what I can expect to feel in the days to follow. "You may experience sharp pains around the affected area. Don't worry. That's normal." Then, when the pain comes, I know not to call the doctor or run to the hospital. I just need to ride out the painful episodes, knowing they will eventually subside and then disappear completely.

Paul reassures the believers in Rome, in effect, "You may experience hardship from the world or even persecution from nonbelievers. Don't worry. That's normal."

—8:37–39—

Believing and accepting grace does not come naturally to the flesh; therefore we must do now what we did in the beginning: Know the truth, reckon the truth, and apply the truth as we depend on the Holy Spirit to keep us connected to the Father.

"In all these things …" (8:37). What things? Everything the Christian experiences. From the initial elation of emancipation, to the sobering reality of freedom, to the realization that our old slave master will not let us go so easily, to the struggle with the flesh, to the persecution of the world. The joys, the sorrows, the setbacks, and triumphs—all of it. In all these things we, the sheep, conquer.

The image of sheep overcoming and conquering an enemy is laughable! Fighting sheep? Not really. We conquer because we have a champion, Jesus—who is the "Lamb of God" but is also the "Lion of Judah." The Suffering Servant in the book of Isaiah the prophet is also the conquering king of the Psalms and the book of Revelation. We will be victorious because He will win the victory on our behalf.

Writing with full apostolic authority, Paul declares, "I am persuaded …" His words in Greek mean "I stand convinced" (8:38). The verb is a Greek perfect tense, indicating that something occurred in the past with ongoing results to the present time. He was convinced that nothing in life, or even our archenemy, death, can keep the love of Christ from us. His own death and resurrection reveal His power over anything and everything that threatens us in the natural realm. Furthermore, nothing in the supernatural realm—including angels (elect or fallen) and spiritual forces—can harm us. God created all things, including everything in the supernatural realm, and He continues to rule over His universe.

Because God rules over everything in time and space, nothing can subvert His will, which is to bring His people to Himself, cleanse us of sin inside and out, shape us into the image of Christ, restore us to life, and allow us to enjoy "peace with God" forever.

Paul began this major section with a penetrating question. "Are we to continue in sin?" (6:1). In other words, now that we have been emancipated from slavery to sin, shall we continue to serve sin as before? The obvious answer is a resounding "No!" However, sin will not give up its slaves easily. The battle persists.

On August 26, 1863, several months after the Emancipation Proclamation had taken effect, President Lincoln reassured the nation with a word picture from Herman Melville's *Moby Dick*. "We are like whalers who have been on a long chase: we have at last got the harpoon into the monster, but we must now look how we steer, or with one 'flop' of his tail he will send us all into eternity."[13]

I'm ready for eternity. I have nothing to fear in the life to come. But learning to live in the freedom of God's grace will come neither naturally nor easily. Fortunately, my God has His harpoon in the monster. Slaying him is only a matter of time.

Application

Mark These Words

I have no idea what challenge you are facing today or what sorrow weighs heavily on your heart. Chances are good that few, if any, know about your struggle. And if they do, no one can appreciate the complexity, the absurdity, the hopelessness of that burden—a difficulty words cannot adequately describe. In many ways we are not free to share it with others because, in truth, no one can fully enter our sorrow, despite their best efforts to understand. We welcome whatever fleeting moments of empathy we encounter, but they fail to satisfy.

You would expect me to say this; nevertheless I must because it is true: *God knows.*

It is a great truth of Scripture that God knows everything. He is omniscient. God is not discovering, God is not learning, God is not watching and then adapting His plan to fit what might help make us comfortable. His plan is set. His knowledge is thorough. He gives purpose to every chaotic circumstance of this fallen, corrupted world. Moreover, He loves us completely—more than any one can love us, even ourselves. Therefore, we can rest in His plan. As musician Michael W. Smith said in a recent concert, "God is still God and I'm still not."

In my experience, submitting my trials to the sovereign plan of God and embracing His providence over all earthly matters are a process.

Rejection. Initially, we refuse to accept the injustice or the absurdity or the finality of our difficulty, and we throw our whole selves against it. To beat it down, we will exhaust every financial, emotional, intellectual, and relational resource. We search every crevice of life for an honorable escape ... and then we consider the ones that are not so honorable. The notion that this affliction might, in fact, be the sovereign plan of God is a detestable, unthinkable thought.

Toleration. Progressively, as circumstances either drag on or grow worse, we begin to entertain the possibility that God may not miraculously intervene, that He might leave the affliction in place. Frustration, outrage, pleading, negotiating, seeking purpose, and further attempts to escape our pain eventually dissolve into a despairing sadness. We struggle less under the crushing weight of God's sovereign plan, resigned to make the best of a future that cannot be avoided.

Epiphany. Gradually, we begin to see glimmers of God's purpose, a silver lining as some have called it. Having long ago surrendered our will to His sovereign plan—though with sulking hopelessness—we accept His providence, little by little. We gather scraps of joy from here and there, and before we know it, life becomes enriching. Our affliction has changed from an unwanted enemy to an indispensable part of who we have become. A sorrowful but vital addition. Then, one day, we see it. The purpose. We perceive with sweet sadness how the affliction was necessary for us to receive the blessings we now enjoy and how the plan of God could have taken no other path.

You might recognize a familiar pattern in the process of submission to God's plan. Elisabeth Kübler-Ross called this process "the stages of grief" in her book *On Death and Dying*: denial, anger, bargaining, depression, and acceptance. But don't mistake this natural ability to recover from tragedy for the supernatural working of the Holy Spirit. Yes, sooner or later, we will reach the final stage of "acceptance," but only God can transform us and only God will give us spiritual insight. Many unbelievers come to terms with the calamities they face, but they rarely emerge whole. Believers, however, become like the Son of God: "Although He was a Son, He learned obedience from the things which He suffered" (Heb. 5:8).

I want to encourage you to do something unusual. Open your Bible to Romans 8:28–39. Think of a word (or two) that best encapsulates the one struggle you face now, the affliction that makes your life miserable, which you would do almost anything to remove. Draw a bracket in the margin of your Bible alongside 8:28–39 and then note your affliction along the bracket.

For the next few days, place your Bible somewhere close to where you will be during the day and keep it open to this passage. Read it periodically and, each time, pray. Pray that the promises of this passage will penetrate your mind. Pray that the Holy Spirit will heal your wounds and teach you both trust and submission. Pray that your affliction will end, but then quickly surrender control to God's way.

I would not presume to tell you how things will unfold for you, nor do I dare suggest the path to obedience will be short or easy. On the contrary! But I can promise you this: This page from your Bible with the words you write next to Romans 8:28–39 will one day become a treasure for you. You will reflect back on this time and you will realize how far you have come ... and you will not want to trade anything for the richness of God's blessing you will have received.

NOTES: The Faithfulness of God (Romans 6:1–8:39)

1. Booker T. Washington, *Up from Slavery* (New York: Doubleday, 1901), 19–20.

2. Ibid., 20.

3. Gerhard Kittel and Gerhard Friedrich, eds., *Theological Dictionary of the New Testament: Abridged in One Volume*, trans. Geoffrey W. Bromiley (Grand Rapids: Eerdmans, 1985), 180.

4. Warren W. Wiersbe, *The Bible Exposition Commentary* (Wheaton, IL: Victor Books, 1989), comment on Rom. 6:1.

5. Jesus came close when He contrasted humanity's standard of judgment and God's (see John 8:15).

6. Ralph Erskine, *Sermons and Other Practical Works* (Falkirk: Peter Muirhead, Rev. John Stewart, and Hugh Mitchell, Publishers, 1796), 7:275.

7. Please, no letters from West Texas. I am a Texan and I love *all* of Texas. My illustration is not intended to suggest that my friends out there are lost and living in misery! It's hot, but it isn't Hell!

8. Greek syntax frequently drops verbs in a couplet with the understanding that they are the same as the first line.

9. Donald Grey Barnhouse, *Exposition of Bible Doctrines, Taking the Epistle to the Romans As a Point of Departure* (Grand Rapids: Eerdmans, 1955), 3:34.

10. Alan Redpath, *The Making of a Man of God: Studies in the Life of David* (Westwood, NJ: Revell, 1962), 93.

11. F. B. Meyer, *Christ in Isaiah* (London: Morgan and Scott, 1917), 9.

12. A. W. Tozer, *The Root of the Righteous* (Camp Hill, PA: Christian Publications, 1986), 137.

13. Abraham Lincoln, quoted by Doris Kearns Godwin in *Team of Rivals* (New York: Simon and Schuster, 2005), 688.

HOW TO BEGIN A RELATIONSHIP WITH GOD

Nobody can live free from the bondage of sin, discover purpose in suffering, or partake of the promises of God's providence without having first experienced the supernatural work of God through a personal relationship with Jesus Christ. But once a person has begun a relationship with God, he or she will be forever identified with Christ, dead to sin, alive to God, granted power from on high, and included in God's eternal promises of glory. But what, exactly, does it mean to begin a relationship with God? How does a person take this crucial first step?

Let's take a look at what Scripture says about this life-giving relationship. The Bible marks the path to God with four essential truths. We'll look at each marker in detail.

Our Spiritual Condition: Totally Depraved

The first truth is rather personal. One look in the mirror of Scripture, and our human condition becomes painfully clear:

> "There is none righteous, not even one;
> There is none who understands,
> There is none who seeks for God;
> All have turned aside, together they have become useless;
> There is none who does good,
> There is not even one." (Romans 3:10–12)

We are all sinners through and through—totally depraved. Now, that doesn't mean we've committed every atrocity known to humankind. We're not as *bad* as we can be, just as *bad off* as we can be. Sin colors all our thoughts, motives, words, and actions.

You still don't believe it? Look around. Everything around us bears the smudge marks of our sinful nature. Despite our best efforts to create a perfect world, crime statistics continue to soar, divorce rates keep climbing, and families keep crumbling.

Something has gone terribly wrong in our society and in ourselves—something deadly. Contrary to how the world would repackage it, "me-first" living doesn't equal rugged individuality and freedom; it equals death. As Paul said in his letter to the Romans, "The wages of sin is death" (Romans 6:23)—our spiritual and physical death that comes from God's righteous judgment of our sin, along with all of the emotional and practical effects of this separation that we experience on a daily basis. This brings us to the second marker: God's character.

God's Character: Infinitely Holy

How can God judge us for a sinful state we were born into? Our total depravity is only half the answer. The other half is God's infinite holiness.

The fact that we know things are not as they should be points us to a standard of goodness beyond ourselves. Our sense of injustice in life on this side of eternity implies a perfect standard of justice beyond our reality. That standard and source is God Himself. And God's standard of holiness contrasts starkly with our sinful condition.

Scripture says that "God is Light, and in Him there is no darkness at all" (1 John 1:5). God is absolutely holy—which creates a problem for us. If He is so pure, how can we who are so impure relate to Him?

Perhaps we could try being better people, try to tilt the balance in favor of our good deeds, or seek out methods for self-improvement. Throughout history, people have attempted to live up to God's standard by keeping the Ten Commandments or living by their own code of ethics. Unfortunately, no one can come close to satisfying the demands of God's law. Romans 3:20 says, "By the works of the Law no flesh will be justified in His sight; for through the Law comes the knowledge of sin."

Our Need: A Substitute

So here we are, sinners by nature and sinners by choice, trying to pull ourselves up by our own bootstraps to attain a relationship with our holy Creator. But every time we try, we fall flat on our faces. We can't live a good enough life to make up for our sin, because God's standard isn't "good enough"—it's *perfection*. And we can't make amends for the offense our sin has created without dying for it.

Who can get us out of this mess?

If someone could live perfectly, honoring God's law, and would bear sin's death penalty for us—in our place—then we would be saved from our predicament. But is there such a person? Thankfully, yes!

Meet your substitute—*Jesus Christ*. He is the One who took death's place for you!

> [God] made [Jesus Christ] who knew no sin to be sin on our behalf, so that we might become the righteousness of God in Him. (2 Corinthians 5:21)

God's Provision: A Savior

God rescued us by sending His Son, Jesus, to die on the cross for our sins (1 John 4:9–10). Jesus was fully human and fully divine (John 1:1, 18), a truth that ensures His understanding of our weaknesses, His power to forgive, and His ability to bridge the gap between God and us (Romans 5:6–11). In short, we are "justified as a gift by His grace through the redemption which is in Christ Jesus" (Romans 3:24). Two words in this verse bear further explanation: *justified* and *redemption.*

Justification is God's act of mercy, in which He declares righteous the believing sinners while we are still in our sinning state. Justification doesn't mean that God *makes* us righteous, so that we never sin again, rather that He *declares* us righteous—much like a judge pardons a guilty criminal. Because Jesus took our sin upon Himself and suffered our judgment on the cross, God forgives our debt and proclaims us PARDONED.

Redemption is Christ's act of paying the complete price to release us from sin's bondage. God sent His Son to bear His wrath for all of our sins—past, present, and future (Romans 3:24–26; 2 Corinthians 5:21). In humble obedience, Christ willingly endured the shame of the cross for our sake (Mark 10:45; Romans 5:6–8; Philippians 2:8). Christ's death satisfied God's righteous demands. He no longer holds our sins against us, because His own Son paid the penalty for them. We are freed from the slave market of sin, never to be enslaved again!

Placing Your Faith in Christ

These four truths describe how God has provided a way to Himself through Jesus Christ. Because the price has been paid in full by God, we must respond to His free gift of eternal life in total faith and confidence in Him to save us. We must step forward into the relationship with God that He has prepared for us—not by doing good works or by being a good person, but by coming to Him just as we are and accepting His justification and redemption by faith.

> For by grace you have been saved through faith; and that not of your-selves, it is the gift of God; not as a result of works, so that no one may boast. (Ephesians 2:8–9)

We accept God's gift of salvation simply by placing our faith in Christ alone for the forgiveness of our sins. Would you like to enter a relationship with your Creator by trusting in Christ as your Savior? If so, here's a simple prayer you can use to express your faith:

> *Dear God,*
> *I know that my sin has put a barrier between You and me. Thank You for sending Your Son, Jesus, to die in my place. I trust in Jesus alone to forgive my sins, and I accept His gift of eternal life. I ask Jesus to be my personal Savior and the Lord of my life. Thank You. In Jesus's name, amen.*

If you've prayed this prayer or one like it and you wish to find out more about knowing God and His plan for you in the Bible, contact us at Insight for Living. Our contact information is on the following pages.

WE ARE HERE FOR YOU

If you desire to find out more about knowing God and His plan for you in the Bible, contact us. Insight for Living provides staff pastors who are available for free written correspondence or phone consultation. These seminary-trained and seasoned counselors have years of experience and are well-qualified guides for your spiritual journey.

Please feel welcome to contact your regional Pastoral Ministries by using the information below:

United States
Insight for Living
Pastoral Ministries
Post Office Box 269000
Plano, Texas 75026-9000
USA
972-473-5097, Monday through Friday,
8:00 a.m. – 5:00 p.m. Central time
www.insight.org/contactapastor

Canada
Insight for Living Canada
Pastoral Ministries
Post Office Box 2510
Vancouver, BC V6B 3W7
CANADA
1-800-663-7639
info@insightforliving.ca

Australia, New Zealand, and South Pacific
Insight for Living Australia
Pastoral Care
Post Office Box 443
Boronia, VIC 3155
AUSTRALIA
1 300 467 444

United Kingdom and Europe
Insight for Living United Kingdom
Pastoral Care
Post Office Box 348
Leatherhead
KT22 2DS
UNITED KINGDOM
0800 915 9364
+44 (0) 1372 370 055
pastoralcare@insightforliving.org.uk

ORDERING INFORMATION

If you would like to order other Insight for Living resources, please contact the office that serves you.

United States
Insight for Living
Post Office Box 269000
Plano, Texas 75026-9000
USA
1-800-772-8888 (Monday through Friday, 7:00 a.m. – 7:00 p.m. Central time)
www.insight.org
www.insightworld.org

Canada
Insight for Living Canada
Post Office Box 2510
Vancouver, BC V6B 3W7
CANADA
1-800-663-7639
www.insightforliving.ca

Australia, New Zealand, and South Pacific
Insight for Living Australia
Post Office Box 443
Boronia, VIC 3155
AUSTRALIA
1 300 467 444
www.insight.asn.au

United Kingdom and Europe
Insight for Living United Kingdom
Post Office Box 348
Leatherhead
KT22 2DS
UNITED KINGDOM
0800 915 9364
www.insightforliving.org.uk

Other International Locations
International constituents may contact the U.S. office through our Web site (www.insightworld.org), mail queries, or by calling +1-972-473-5136.

More on Romans 6–8 from Insight for Living

Living as God desires in a world gone astray is not always as easy as it sounds. Fortunately, God reveals in His Word the principles we need in order to follow Him faithfully. This Bible Companion, covering Romans 6–8, integrates five inspiring DVD messages from Chuck Swindoll with ten practical lessons for individual or group study. In this series, you'll explore such life-changing topics as:

- Winning your battle against habitual sin.
- Squaring off against legalistic dos and don'ts.
- Persevering in spite of suffering.
- Trusting in God's providence.

The pressures to conform to secular ideals seem more urgent every day. But applying the truths of Romans 6–8 to your life will dramatically strengthen your relationship with God. Take advantage of this series today, and begin to experience *Supernatural Living in a Secular World.*

www.insight.org • www.insightworld.org
For ordering information, see pages 85–86.